From Darkness to Light

How One Became a Christian in the Early Church

by Anne Field, O.S.B.

EXORCISM 20, 26, 28, 29, 31, 78
DOORKEEPER, 22

OPENING OF THE EARS, 133, 137

Conciliar Press
Ben Lomond, California

FROM DARKNESS TO LIGHT
© 1978, 1997 by Anne Field, O.S.B.
All Rights Reserved

Formerly published by Servant Publications (ISBN 0-89283-061-1)
Published in England under the title *New Life* by A.R. Mowbray & Co.
Ltd., Oxford, 1980

Published by   Conciliar Press
                P.O. Box 76
                Ben Lomond, California 95005-0076

Printed in the United States of America
ISBN 1-888212-06-3

Cover photo by Dan Agulian

Library of Congress Cataloging-in-Publication Data

Field, Anne.
    From darkness to light : how one became a Christian in the
early church / by Anne Field.
        p.   cm.
    Includes bibliographical references and index.
    ISBN 1-888212-06-3
    1. Catechumens—History. 2. Catechumens—Religious life.
3. Catechetics—History—Early church, ca. 30–600. 4. Initiation rites—Religious aspects—Christianity—History of doctrines—Early church, ca. 30–600.   5. Mystagogy—
Christianity—History.
I. Title.
BR195.C38F54   1997
268'.09'015—dc21   97-16511
                                                        CIP

Table of Contents

Note to the Present Edition

When Conciliar Press suggested the publication of a new edition of these ancient patristic teachings, which belong to our common Christian patrimony, I was very grateful for the opportunity, since the book has been found useful in many Western churches as an accompaniment to the Lenten program of preparation for baptism or reception into the Church at Easter, and it is still in frequent demand. It is an added joy to share this tradition with our Orthodox brothers and sisters who also draw inspiration from the same sources.

I should like to express my gratitude to Deacon R. Thomas Zell of Conciliar Press and his associate editor, Katherine Hyde, for their helpful and courteous suggestions.

Sister Anne Field, O.S.B.
Stanbrook Abbey, England
March, 1997

Foreword

In the stillness of an ancient church, early Christians pray throughout the long hours of the night. With them stand the "newly illumined," whose intensive preparation has at last been rewarded with baptism into Christ. Together all will greet the dawning of the new morning—the culmination of the greatest and oldest celebration of the Christian Church: Holy Pascha.

As the Apostle John wrote, "God is light and in Him there is no darkness at all." This same theme may be seen from beginning to end in the writings of St. John, who never lets us forget that Christ is "the true Light, which gives light to every man coming into the world." There is no wonder then that in preparing new converts for entry, the Church from the very beginning emphasized that they were coming from darkness to light.

St. John Chrysostom, in his baptismal instructions, speaks of the brightness of the baptismal robe clothing the newly baptized: "Your shining robe now arouses admiration in the eyes of all who behold you, and the radiance of your garments demonstrates that your souls are free from every blemish." Within these instructions he continually reminds his hearers of the words of Christ: "Let your light so shine before men that they may see your good works and glorify your Father in heaven" (Matt. 5:16).

This light, he tells them, does not stop with the bodily senses, but illumines the soul and understanding of those who see it— and after it dispels the darkness of evil, it draws those who find it to shine with their own light (received and reflected from Christ the Light) and to imitate the life of virtue.

Not only, then, does a virtuous life improve the lot of the one who lives it, but it also, by its brilliance, draws others to the Savior and moves them to praise God. Baptismal instruction concerning this great truth is to be found not only in the writings of John Chrysostom, but within the teachings of all the Church Fathers.

Here, then, is a compilation of early Church teachings on this most basic of Christian sacraments—baptism into Christ. Anne Field has drawn from the ancient writers of the undivided Church—taking us back to a time when there was One Holy Catholic and Apostolic Church in East and West. Here we find teachings from Fathers of the third to fifth centuries from across the Christian world, such as Ambrose of Milan, Augustine of Hippo, Cyprian of Carthage, Cyril of Jerusalem, Didymus the Blind of Alexandria, John Chrysostom of Constantinople, and others. Anne's choices were difficult for one reason only: there are so many from whom to choose.

Let us therefore enter in, join with the catechumens of the early undivided Church, and learn once again what it means to become a Christian, to be incorporated into Christ. Let us receive instruction with them in the great mysteries of our timeless Faith. And let us keep vigil, pondering anew that prophetic word spoken throughout the ages, "which you do well to heed as a light that shines in a dark place, until the day dawns and the morning star rises in your hearts" (2 Peter 1:19).

Jack N. Sparks
Elk Grove, California

Introduction

When Saint Paul lists the different charisms* with which the Lord endowed His Church in order that all its members might work together to build up the Body of Christ (Eph. 4:11, 12), he makes a distinction between the ministry of the evangelist and that of the pastor or teacher. It is one thing to preach the Good News and convert unbelievers to Christianity; it is another to prepare new converts for baptism.*

The Church has always attached great importance to the task of the catechist,* insisting that converts receive a thorough explanation of the Christian Faith and way of life. But teaching methods have varied over the centuries. Though the Faith is one and the same, there is a great difference between the way it was presented to newcomers in the first five hundred years of the Church's life and the way converts have been instructed in more recent times.

We are not told how long it took the Apostle Philip to evangelize the Ethiopian eunuch as he sat beside him in his chariot on the road to Gaza. The impression given by the account in the Acts of the Apostles is that after a couple of hours, Philip judged

---

*Terms or practices which may be unfamiliar to some readers are marked with an asterisk and explained in the Glossary beginning on p. 238.

that the eunuch was ready for baptism. The eunuch was, of course, already acquainted with the Jewish Scriptures and a worshipper of the God of Israel; the Apostle only had to show him how all the Old Testament prophecies had been fulfilled in Jesus Christ.

But as the gospel spread to large numbers of pagans, catechetical instruction* required more time. Saint Luke says that Paul and Barnabas spent a year at Antioch, instructing a large number of people (Acts 11:26). Not only did these applicants need to be taught the basic truths of creation, sin, and redemption, but they also had to renounce their former idolatry and superstitious practices.

Very soon the Church developed a structured system of preparation for baptism in which doctrinal teaching and moral testing were accompanied by various symbolic rites. Written records of these early catechetical instructions are few and incomplete until we come to the patristic writings of the fourth and fifth centuries, when the number of adult converts was at its peak and the discipline of the catechumenate* thoroughly established.

A considerable amount of scholarly work has been devoted to the early catechumenate and the rites of Christian initiation. Critical texts and commentaries on the more important baptismal homilies surviving from the second to the fifth century have been published and are of the greatest service to students of the liturgy* and the Church Fathers. This book owes much to them, but is intended less for students than for readers who are seeking to deepen their understanding of the new life and spiritual power that was given them at their own baptism and chrismation.* It is an attempt to reconstruct the catechetical instructions of the second half of the fourth century and beginning of the fifth in such a way as to present a complete course of teaching, extending from the beginning of Lent,* when the candidates gave in their names for baptism at Easter (Orthodox Pascha),* until the end of the week following Easter (Orthodox Bright Week).*

Since details of the ceremonies and the order of explaining them varied from place to place at that time, the series of rites described here is a composite. Some elements not universally observed have been omitted, for example the footwashing* practiced in some regions immediately after baptism. The position of the several anointings has also been streamlined. Similarly it has been necessary to choose between varying explanations of some of the ceremonies. However, the overall impression given by the texts that have come down to us is that a strong unanimity existed among catechists throughout the Church, pointing to a common tradition going back to apostolic times. Just as the Apostles based their preaching on Jesus Christ as the fulfillment of the Scriptures, so the ancient catechetical teachings are based on the principle that the realities of the Old Testament prefigure the realities of the New, having been fulfilled in Christ and in the sacraments of the New Covenant.

When we compare these early baptismal instructions with a more recent approach to catechetics,* one of the first things that impresses us is their biblical foundation. We are also struck by the corporate character of Christian initiation, and the vivid use of symbolic actions in the rites.

Conversion is thought of in terms of engagement in the tremendous drama of redemption, in which God is the principal actor who snatches men and women away from the powers of darkness in order to bring them into the Kingdom of His beloved Son. The other main role belongs to Satan, the Adversary. The candidate finds himself solicited by two opposing forces, and must freely choose to which of them he will give his allegiance. If he chooses Christ, he must from that point on fight against the devil. He must enlist as a soldier of Christ and prepare for spiritual combat. But he is not alone in this battle.

The Church fights with him. Baptism is never a purely individual or family affair; it concerns the entire Christian community, who support the candidate during his time of probation by their prayers and fasting.* When he is baptized, the new Christian becomes a member of a living body.

His initiation is effected by means of a series of symbolic actions that speak to the whole person—body, mind, and soul—far more powerfully than words alone could ever do. In this way the candidate apprehends the truths imparted to him not as abstractions but as concrete realities. For the rest of his life the experience of his entrance into the Church will remain impressed on his memory.

Today, of course, the average church does not have hundreds of converts from paganism to prepare for baptism each year. There are, however, many Christians to whom baptism meant very little until the Holy Spirit touched their lives, so that their first real commitment to following Christ was made only after many years of belonging to a Christian church. This commitment has led to such a change in their lives that many of them consider themselves "new Christians." They are eager to learn more about life in the Spirit and to appropriate the grace of the sacraments they received so long ago. The catechetical instructions of the early Church may, I hope, speak to their needs.

The main sources used here are the *Catechetical and Mystagogical Lectures* of Saint Cyril of Jerusalem and, according to some scholars, his successor John; the *Catechetical Homilies* of Theodore of Mopsuestia; the two treatises *On the Sacraments* and *On the Mysteries* by Saint Ambrose; the *Baptismal Catecheses* of Saint John Chrysostom; and the *Sermons* of Saint Augustine. Representing dioceses in Palestine, Syria, northern Italy, and North Africa, they show us a cross-section of the Church in patristic times. A few paragraphs and sentences from other early

Church Fathers have also been woven into the fabric, but form only a small part of the whole.

From these materials I have tried to assemble a series of instructions which capture something of the lively extemporaneous style of the original addresses. Sources for each section are indicated at the end of the book and an index has been included to identify the particular Father from whose work each section is drawn. (The abbreviations used in these notes are explained in the biographical information on page 226.) But in a nontechnical undertaking such as this, it seemed better to avoid distracting the reader with a large number of footnotes and detailed references. The texts have been translated very freely, edited, paraphrased, abridged or amplified, in whatever way would serve best to convey the teaching by which the Fathers, using every skill at their command, endeavored to instill the Christian Faith into the minds and hearts of their audience.

Since each teacher left his personal stamp on the ancient catechetical tradition, a synthesis such as this will inevitably contain a mixture of styles. However, the Fathers themselves were happily unconcerned about mixing their images and metaphors. Saint Ambrose often leaps from one idea to another, Theodore is almost unbelievably long-winded, Saint John Chrysostom frequently pursues red herrings—all of which shows that their instructions were given extempore, and were often interrupted by questions from the class. Someone present took notes of what was said, and so preserved it for posterity. The teacher himself may have worked over the notes later, but his many labors and responsibilities did not always allow him to do so. Consequently I am not too worried over inconsistencies of style, since I am in good company.

A more intractable problem has been the disposition of the material over the weeks of Lent and Easter week. We learn from that untiring fourth-century pilgrim to the holy places, the nun

Egeria, that in Jerusalem the baptismal candidates received three hours' teaching every day during Lent.

"During these forty days," she writes enthusiastically to her sisters at home, "the bishop goes through the whole of the Bible, beginning with Genesis. First he teaches the literal meaning of each passage, then he gives its spiritual interpretation. He also teaches them about the resurrection and everything concerning the faith (i.e., the teaching of the New Testament). This is called *catechesis.*

"After five weeks of this teaching he gives them the Creed, explaining it article by article just as he explained the scriptures. This means that all the people in this part of the world are able to follow the scripture readings in church, since there has been three hours' catechesis on all the scriptures from six to nine in the morning throughout the whole of Lent."[1]

Obviously it is not possible here to reproduce a hundred and twenty hours of scripture lessons. In any case, the Jerusalem Catechesis that has come down to us comprises only nineteen lectures before baptism and five during the following week. The greater part of the Lenten instructions contained in it is an extended explanation of the Creed, with scriptural proofs. Like Theodore's *Catechetical Homilies,* these instructions include many arguments designed to arm the candidates against the heresies of the day. These, being of less profit to us, have been omitted.

Extensive scripture study was also part of the catechetical instruction in other cities. Saint Ambrose refers to the "lives of the patriarchs and the maxims of the book of Proverbs"[2] which he has been expounding in Milan during Lent. It would seem that his books on Abraham, Cain, Elijah, and other biblical figures contain the substance of his Lenten sermons. In North Africa, Saint Augustine preached at the daily Lenten eucharistic liturgy.* These public sermons, which were attended by the catechumens,* counted as an important part of their instruction, but they are not included here.

The preachers occasionally make mysterious allusions to matters "which the baptized will understand." These remarks refer to the discipline of secrecy in regard to the central mysteries* of the Christian Faith, which catechumens were not allowed to hear. Explanations of the Eucharist* were invariably reserved until after baptism; in many places those of baptism and chrismation were similarly reserved. Egeria reports that at the beginning of Holy Week the bishop tells the candidates:

"During the past seven weeks you have been given instruction in the whole of scripture. You have been taught about the Christian faith and the resurrection of the body, and you have also learned as much as catechumens are allowed to know of the meaning of the Creed. But the teaching on baptism itself is much deeper, and as long as you remain catechumens you have no right to hear it. However, do not think it will never be explained to you. You will be told everything after you have been baptized. But catechumens cannot be told about God's secret mysteries."[3]

Unlike the bishop of Jerusalem, Theodore and John Chrysostom do explain the meaning of the baptismal rite beforehand, and I have followed their example in order to reduce the quantity of teaching to be fitted into Easter week, since many more of the so-called mystagogical addresses have survived than the prebaptismal ones (the term *mystagogic* indicates sacramental teaching).

Rather than allocate a portion of the instructions to each day of the entire period in an artificial manner, it seemed preferable to group them under the following headings:

I   The bishop's opening address to the baptismal candidates on the first Monday of Lent.

II Explanation of the basic gospel message during the first four weeks of Lent. (In this section I would ask the reader not only to assume the existence of supplementary lectures which it would be tedious to reproduce *in extenso,* but also, both here and in the following sections, to allow for a longer or shorter period of time according to the day on which it was customary to hold the giving and rendering of the Creed and Lord's Prayer, the scrutiny, the renunciation and initial sealing in different regions. A very useful summary of all these variations is provided by Fr. Edward Yarnold S.J. in his excellent study, *The Awe-Inspiring Rites of Initiation.*)

III The Giving of the Creed on the Fourth Sunday of Lent and throughout the following week.

IV The Scrutiny, Rendering of the Creed, and Giving of the Lord's Prayer on the Fifth Sunday of Lent and following days.

V Explanation of the baptismal rites during the last week of Lent and beginning of Holy Week.

VI The rites of initiation on Holy Saturday and during the Easter vigil.

VII Postbaptismal instructions during Easter week.

A personal testimony to the effects of baptism by Saint Cyprian, the third-century martyr and bishop of Carthage, has been added. Although Cyprian lived before the time of these catechetical lectures, his witness is so relevant to them that it makes an appropriate epilogue. Finally, an appendix shows the method used in constructing this book, and discusses the patristic teaching on the different senses of Scripture.

Working on these ancient writings has meant coming to know the men whose teaching they embody, entering into the experience of their hearers, and sharing their gratitude to God for His inexpressible gift. May those who read this book also derive inspiration from their fellow Christians of the past.

I
THE BISHOP'S
OPENING ADDRESS

Chapter One

During the first Christian centuries, baptism figured prominently in the life of the Church. Year after year, crowds of new believers flocked to be enrolled for the sacrament. The Church's rejoicing over Christ's victory at Easter was enhanced by the solemn baptism of the candidates who had appropriated this victory for themselves. And in the life of each Christian, baptism was the culmination of years of eager preparation; it was his resurrection to new life.

In the third century, each candidate for baptism went through a three-year period of probation, known as the catechumenate. Stringent conditions were attached to admission; the Church did not want halfhearted Christians who might endanger her principles. Applicants were examined regarding their motives, their condition in life, and their morals. Certain occupations were considered incompatible with Christianity; these included anything connected with pagan worship, the theater, or the gladiatorial games. Even spectators at such displays were excluded. Soldiers were not admitted, since they had to swear an oath to a pagan emperor and were often obliged to execute unjust orders; nor were officials of the state, because they could not avoid taking part in pagan rites. Even artists and teachers were treated with great reserve, since their work usually involved depicting the pagan gods and explaining pagan literature.

The three years of the catechumenate were a period of moral testing, a sort of religious novitiate,* accompanied by a regular course of instructions. The candidates were allowed to be present at the first part of the eucharistic liturgy, now called the Synaxis or Liturgy of the Word* but formerly known as the Liturgy of the Catechumens. After the sermon they were dismissed. They were also given special teaching on Scripture from catechists, who paid particular attention to the moral lessons to be drawn from the biblical texts.

At the end of the three years an enquiry was made into the conduct of the candidates during their probation. Those who proved ready then received several weeks of intensive preparation for baptism at Easter. During these weeks they were instructed in the whole course of salvation history, the Old Testament prophecies and their fulfillment in Christ, the life and Passion of Jesus Christ, and the good news of redemption. The Apostles' Creed* was systematically explained to the candidates, who were required to learn it by heart so that before their baptism they could each recite it in the presence of the bishop. They were also initiated into many Christian practices; they were obliged to fast, to pray on their knees, and to keep night vigils.* Exorcisms were pronounced over them daily, in order that the devil's power over them might be gradually weakened and broken.*

During Holy Week the candidates were told to wash themselves in readiness for the sacrament, and to spend Friday and Saturday in strict fasting.* The sacraments* of baptism, chrismation, and the Eucharist were administered during the Easter vigil, and then, during the whole of the following week, the bishop explained to the newly baptized the meaning of what they had received. It was held that the full meaning of the sacraments could only be grasped by means of the grace of enlightenment they themselves imparted.

Children of Christian parents were baptized at the same time as adults. During the fourth century, however, parents often delayed to bring their children to the font; in fact many people began to defer the reception of baptism until they were on their deathbed. By so doing they could avoid many of the obligations of the faithful. They also calculated that by being baptized at the last moment, they could go to eternity still in their baptismal innocence. This practice became common after the end of the third century. The Church opposed it strenuously, stressing the danger of sudden death, and before the beginning of each Lent bishops urged the catechumens in their congregations to give in their names for baptism without delay.

In view of this development, however, the course of teaching given during the earlier three-year probationary period could no longer be maintained in the fourth and fifth centuries. Consequently a new method was devised, whereby a single preliminary instruction was given to anyone applying for admission to the catechumenate, consisting of a summary outline of the faith and conduct required of a Christian. At his enrollment the catechumen was marked with the sign of the cross on his forehead and received a symbolic administration of blessed salt; then the catechist breathed in his face commanding the unclean spirit to depart. The catechumen was finally dismissed with the laying on of hands and a prayer of blessing. After this he was left to himself, perhaps for many years, until he reported for baptism at the beginning of Lent. During this Lent he underwent the same proximate preparation for the sacraments that the Church had always given, though it was now more intensive since the candidate had not had the benefit of the earlier catechetical teaching.

Those who sought baptism had to find sponsors* to vouch for them, and it was necessary for any whose homes were in distant parts of the diocese to find lodgings in the city during the whole of Lent and Easter week in order to attend the daily instructions. Names had to be given in before the first Sunday of Lent.

21

On the morning of the first Monday of Lent the candidates entered the church with their sponsors, filing past the doorkeepers, who scrutinized them as they came in. They were brought one by one before the bishop, who enquired into their manner of life and worthiness of admission. If he received satisfactory answers from the witnesses, the bishop himself wrote the candidate's name in the register. But if it transpired that any catechumen was leading a disorderly or immoral life, he was dismissed and told to mend his ways before he could come forward for baptism.

When all the candidates had been examined, stewards instructed them to sit in a semicircle round the bishop's chair. Their sponsors were given a place behind them, and any of the faithful who wanted to listen—except catechumens who had not enrolled—were allowed to be present. When all were settled in their places, the bishop began his opening address.

Brothers and sisters, welcome to the Church of God! Not that you are total strangers to the Church; some of you have been catechumens for years now, coming regularly to the first part of the liturgy, hearing the scripture readings, taking part in the prayers, and listening to the sermons. You have already absorbed a good deal of teaching. One might say you have picked an armful of spiritual flowers to weave yourselves heavenly crowns, and have already inhaled the fragrance of the Holy Spirit. But you have put off making the total commitment to Jesus Christ which baptism demands.

Now you have made up your minds. You have given in your names and been enrolled. Your hearts are full of hope and longing, and rightly so; God's word can never deceive you, and in that word it is written: "To those who love God, everything cooperates for good" (Rom. 8:28). God's gifts to us are immeasurable, provided we come to Him with an honest resolve to do our part.

Forgive me if I begin on a note that may sound stern, but I should be failing in my duty if I did not emphasize that you must bring to these instructions a sincere and earnest intention. A person may be physically present at these classes, but if his mind and heart are elsewhere he will get nothing out of them.

Simon the Sorcerer

You remember the story of Simon the Sorcerer in the Acts of the Apostles: how he saw the miraculous powers of the Apostles and the Holy Spirit being given through the laying on of their hands, and how he decided to ask for baptism himself so that he too could enjoy the same power (Acts 8:9–24). The Apostles baptized him, but he was not enlightened; he plunged his body into the water, but he did not open his heart to the light of the Holy Spirit. Although his body went down into the font and came up again, his soul was not buried and raised to life with the Lord Jesus.

I mention this story because, as Saint Paul tells us, these things were written down in Scripture as a lesson to all those who would continue to come to the Church asking for baptism. So then, let none of you here be found tempting God; let none of you join this class merely to satisfy your curiosity. Do not think you can see without being seen; do not imagine you can scrutinize our doings without God scrutinizing your heart while you are about it.

The wedding banquet

We are told in the Gospel about a man who pushed his way into a wedding party unsuitably dressed. Sitting down at table with the other guests, he began to eat, though he observed that they were all dressed for the occasion and knew he should have done the same.

Now the host was a generous man, but he was no fool. As he

moved about among the guests, he asked this man to explain his presence there in soiled, inappropriate clothing. He pointed out that even if he had entered in ignorance of the prescribed dress, he should have learned his mistake when he saw the others. He should have retired and come back suitably clothed. However, since he had come in so unceremoniously, he could be thrown out equally unceremoniously. The host ordered his servants to tie the man up and throw him out into the dark, because he was unworthy of celebrating the wedding with the bridegroom and his guests.

You all know this story; let it be a warning to you. As Christ's ministers, we have admitted everyone to our classes who asked to join. The door was wide open. In doing so, we took the risk that someone might come in with a sin-grimed soul for purposes that were anything but honorable. Now if you are such a person and have entered here and been enrolled without the intention of renouncing all your sinful habits, I earnestly beg you to let the things you see and hear in this place bring you to your senses: the order and discipline of the clergy, the reading of the Scriptures, the presence of the religious, the teachings, and the solemnity of the occasion. Make your escape in good time now, and come back tomorrow in better dispositions. Suppose, for example, your soul is clothed with avarice; when you come back, let it follow a different fashion. Do not simply throw a cloak over your dirty clothes. Strip them off, and put on the clean and presentable dress of good and sober living.

I tell you this now, before Jesus the Bridegroom comes in to inspect your soul. You are allowed forty days to do penance; there is plenty of time for you to discard your soiled garments—that is, to purify your intentions—and put on fresh clothes. Then you can come back again. But if you persist in your wicked purpose, you must not expect to receive any grace. The water may receive you, but the Spirit will not accept you. So then, whoever is aware of having a hidden sore, let him take the remedy for it. Whoever has fallen, let him rise. Let there be no Simon among you, no hypocrisy, no idle curiosity.

The Church's fishing nets

It could be that you had another reason for coming. A man might want to marry a Christian woman, and so come in order to please her. The same could apply to a woman. Someone might want to get on the right side of his employer or to make friends by becoming a Christian.

Well, if you are such a person, perhaps I may use this pretext as an angler's bait and catch you after all! You have come for an inadequate reason, but there is good hope of saving you. You may not have realized what you were letting yourself in for, nor the net that was spread to catch you. My friend, you are now within the Church's fishing nets! Let yourself be caught. Do not try to wriggle out, because Jesus wants to capture you—not to kill you, but to give you new life out of death. For die you must, in order to rise again; you must be dead to sin and alive to holiness (Rom. 6:11). Make up your mind to die to your sins now and begin a new life from this day forward.

You are to receive a divine title

Jesus Christ is offering you a very great honor. Up till now you have been called a catechumen. A catechumen is one who hears without grasping what is promised, one who listens to mysterious things without knowing the depth of meaning contained in them. But when you have been baptized you will no longer hear these things merely with your ears; you will hear them in your hearts, spoken by the indwelling Spirit who is fashioning your soul into a place where God can make His home. When you hear the scripture readings relating to the sacraments, you will understand mysteries of which you have hitherto been ignorant.

Do not think God is offering you some trifling thing. Far from it. You, a mere creature, are to receive a divine title. But take care not to become a Christian in name only. You have entered the lists and engaged in the struggle; run the race while you can, for the chance will not be given you a second time. If you were to be married tomorrow, would you not set aside everything else and prepare for your wedding? You are now about to give your life to the Lord; all the more reason to relinquish unspiritual things in order to take hold of the gifts of the Holy Spirit.

The Lord will see your firm resolve

Baptism can be received only once. With anything else we might hope to do better a second time if we failed at first; but here, if you fail, there is no putting things right.

However, the only thing God asks of us is a good intention. Do not ask me how your sins are going to be blotted out, as if it were some sort of chemical process. I tell you it is by believing and by accepting the forgiveness God offers you in baptism that your sins will be wiped away. I can't put it more plainly than that. You must be fully resolved to renounce all sin and wrongdoing. It is no good saying you are willing if you have reservations in your heart, because the Judge of your actions can read your heart. Here and now, from this moment, break off every evil practice. Guard your tongue from irresponsible talk; keep custody of your eyes to prevent their leading you astray.

Come eagerly to these teaching sessions. Submit to the exorcisms, because their aim is to bring you to salvation. Imagine that you had some gold ore containing a mixture of base substances, and you wanted to extract the pure gold alone. The only way to purge it of foreign substances would be to use fire. In the same way the soul can only be purged of evil by being exorcised. These exorcisms have God's power in them, because they are based on His word. Through their use the enemy is driven out, leaving you with the hope of salvation and eternal life.

Hold on to this hope, my friends; ask the Lord to take control of your lives, and put your trust in Him. If you do this, He will see your firm resolve and cleanse you from your sins, filling you with new hope and granting you the conversion that leads to salvation. He will call you to new life.

The spiritual armor

Persevere with these classes. Even if the lessons are lengthy, do not relax your attention, for they will give you weapons against unbelievers. You have many opponents, and you must be equipped to defend yourselves. An arsenal of weapons is ready for you, and the handiest of them all is the sword of the Spirit. Stretch out your hand and take hold of them—in other words, have a right intention, a determination to fight the Lord's battle, to overcome the devil's wiles, and not to be worsted in any encounter with unbelievers.

Guard the secret

Learn by heart the things that are told you, and guard them always. These instructions are not ordinary sermons such as you hear on Sundays. If you missed one of those, you could hear another the following week. But the teachings before baptism are very carefully prepared, and if you miss one there will be no chance to make it up. You have to be taught about the life of God, about the Judgment, about the Incarnation, about the Resurrection. There is a great deal to be said, and it must be said in the proper order. Each part is connected with the rest; if you do not remember what went before and what came after, your faith will not be firm and sound.

After the class, if any unbeliever or catechumen tries to find out what you have learned, tell him nothing. Guard the secret.

Never let anyone worm it out of you, asking what harm it would do to tell him. I tell you it would do a great deal of harm; it would be like giving a sick person strong drink. Strong drink makes the patient delirious; then he dies and the doctor is blamed. In the same way, if an unbeliever or catechumen hears something divulged by a Christian, he misunderstands and scoffs at it, because there must first be faith before it is possible to understand. And if this should happen, the Christian would be condemned for betraying his trust.

My brothers and sisters, you are standing at the gates of the heavenly mystery. I put you under oath to smuggle nothing out of the citadel, not because the things you are to learn are not fit to be repeated, but because your audience is not ready to understand them. You were once catechumens yourselves, and no one told you the things we are now going to teach you. When you have heard them and grasped their sublimity, you will realize that the uncommitted are not ready for such teachings.

Keep your eyes on the Lord

The sessions will be held every day after Morning Prayers. But first of all each of you should go to the exorcists in turn. If any members are missing, go and look for them. When you are asked out to dinner, do you not wait for your fellow guests? If you have brothers or sisters, do you not want the best for them? So, do all you can to encourage one another. And whatever you do, do not start useless gossip or chatter. Keep your eyes on the Lord; you are going to need His powerful help during the coming weeks. Be still and know that He is God. You may see older Christians adopting a more relaxed attitude in God's house, but they have good reason to relax; they know what they have received and they are in a state of grace. But your future is still in the balance. So do not act as though you were already secure; take every precaution.

When your exorcism is over and while you are waiting for the others, you can read or pray quietly in groups, or discuss among yourselves the things you have been learning. Remember that I shall observe each one's earnestness, each one's devotion. Let all the dross be purged and burned out of your heart; put your soul on the anvil and your doubts under the hammer. Let the rust drop off and leave clean metal. And may the Lord bring you safely through all this long process until we come to Easter night, the night when darkness will be turned into day for you, the night that Scripture says shall be bright as day (Ps. 139:12).

On that night heaven will be opened to each one of you. You will go down into those wonderful Christ-bearing waters; you will receive the name of Christian and the capacity for understanding and appropriating the things of God. So lift up your eyes, think of the angelic choirs and God on His throne ruling the universe, with His beloved Son sitting beside Him, while all the hosts of heaven serve Him and all of you who have been saved share His divine life. Even now imagine you hear the angels singing with joy over your redemption, as you take your place among them, radiant in body and soul.

Beware of the enemy

This baptism which the Church offers you is the greatest possible gift. It brings deliverance to those in bondage and forgiveness to sinners, death to sin and new life for the soul. It is a holy seal, attesting to your new birth as a child of God, a seal that can never be effaced. It is a pledge for you of the Kingdom of heaven and the gift of sonship.

But be warned. There is a dragon lurking beside the road on which you are now walking. Take care he does not bite you and infect you with unbelief. He sees all these crowds of people on the way to salvation, and is determined to devour or obstruct as

many as he can. How are you to get past him safely? I will tell
you: by having your feet shod with the gospel of peace, which
will be a protection against the dragon's bite. By having faith in
your heart, strong hope in your mind, and God's word as a
sword in your hand.

Prepare yourselves to receive instruction and take part in the
sacred mysteries. Pray continually, day and night, that God will
make you fit to receive His new life. If you find sinful suggestions coming into your mind, take refuge in the thought that
God sees and judges all. Study His word and the teaching of the
Church, and temptations will disappear. If anyone makes fun of
your intention to be baptized, you can be sure he is prompted by
the old enemy. Pay no attention to him, but keep your eyes on
the Lord who has called you. Guard your own soul so that you
may not fall into a trap; hold fast to your hope, and you will
inherit eternal salvation.

Only God can bring the work to completion

Now your teachers are only human. It is up to you to turn
their efforts to good account. It is our job to teach you, and
yours to accept what we teach, but only God can bring the work
to completion. We must do all in our power, brace ourselves for
the task, concentrate our minds, and prepare our hearts. Then
we must trust God to do the rest. The race has begun; it is a race
for your soul, and the prize is heaven. Remember that God knows
your hearts and can judge your sincerity. He is powerful enough
to keep honest seekers steadfast and to bring dissemblers to true
faith. If a doubter will only surrender his heart to the Lord, the
Lord can turn him into a sincere believer.

So I pray now that God may blot out the charge that is
written against you (Col. 2:14), and forgive all the sins of your
past life. May He plant you in His Church and make you grow;
may He enroll you in His army and equip you with the armor of

righteousness. And may He fill you with all the spiritual gifts of the New Covenant and give you the indelible seal of the Holy Spirit in Christ Jesus our Lord.

Glory to Him for ever and ever! Amen.

Before the candidates are dismissed, a deacon gives some practical instructions. He announces the place where the daily classes are to be held, and explains that the bishop will not always have time to give the instructions himself, though he will do so on all the principal occasions. A team of catechists will be responsible for the preparation of the candidates; it will include one or two of the priests, deacons, and deaconesses, together with the exorcists.

In addition to the morning sessions, the candidates are exhorted to attend the first part of the daily eucharistic liturgy which, during the Lenten season, is celebrated in the afternoon. In this way they will hear the scripture readings which have been very carefully chosen for these days of preparation for the paschal mystery, and also a sermon each day on the passages just read. These sermons form an important part of the baptismal catechesis, and must be listened to attentively. If anyone is in difficulties, his sponsor will give him extra explanations and help him in every possible way.

Almighty, everlasting God, Father of our Lord Jesus Christ,
look in mercy upon these servants of Yours
whom you have called to knowledge of the Christian Faith.
Take away their blindness of heart;
break the fetters with which Satan has bound them in the
    past;
open to them the door of Your fatherly love.
Let them be initiated into the sacraments Your wisdom has
    devised;
deliver them from the allurements of sin and selfishness
so that they may joyfully follow the sweet fragrance of Your
    commandments within Your Holy Church.
May they make progress each day
until they are ready to receive the grace of Holy Baptism.
We make our prayer through Jesus Christ,
Your only Son, our Lord.
Amen.[4]

II
THE MESSAGE OF
THE GOSPEL

Chapter Two

The Good News is for everyone

My brothers and sisters, I want to begin today by talking about the free gift God is offering His people.

Each of you knows what sort of person he is, and what sort of life he lived in the past. When the Lord called you it was not to settle a score against you, nor to bring you to account for your sins. It was to save you, to forgive you, to offer you new life. In the Gospel Jesus Himself calls out to the whole human race: "Come to Me, all you who are weary and overburdened, and I will give you rest. Take My yoke on your shoulders and learn to imitate Me, for I am meek and humble of heart; then you will find rest for your souls" (Matt. 11:28, 29).

What an invitation! Come to Me, all of you! Not just the powerful, the affluent, the educated, the strong, the healthy, the respectable; but also the weak, the poor, the underprivileged, the sick, the blind, the lame, the disabled, the hopeless, the abandoned. The Master makes no distinction between any of you; the good news is for everyone. Come to Me, He says, all you who toil and groan under your burdens. He is interested especially in those who have squandered their lives, who are weighed down by their sins, who are filled with shame and no longer have any self-respect. These are the ones He calls to Himself, not to punish them, but to comfort their sorrows and ease their heavy load.

For there is no burden more terrible than sin. It crushes us relentlessly, squeezing out joy and peace and life itself. Even if we harden our hearts a thousand times over, even if we succeed in concealing our guilt from the whole world, sin still hangs like a millstone round our necks, our conscience still rises up to confront us. Conscience is a judge we can never bribe; it continually accuses us, tormenting us inwardly, pointing out the enormity of our sins.

If this is the burden which weighs upon you, the Lord's promise is meant for you. Jesus promises to give you rest, by forgiving all your sins. All He asks is that you should come to Him in faith.

Grace is freely offered

Could anyone resist such an appeal? The Kingdom of heaven is offered for sale for the price of faith! Hurry, gather together all your treasures, heap up your gifts of mind and heart, and buy the pearl of great price. And yet when you have done all that, you will discover the pearl is given you for nothing. All that is asked of you is the recognition of the grace that is freely offered. How small an outlay to gain such a prize!

Remember, however, that you yourselves were not purchased so cheaply. God loved you so much that He poured out the precious blood of His only Son for you. Your Father sets great store by you; do not hold yourselves cheap. You will show yourselves worthy of His love if you rid yourselves of all your base qualities and guard what is precious in His eyes; if you serve your Creator instead of creatures; if you refuse to allow your lower nature to rule over you and keep yourselves clean from grave sin.

The New Covenant

God offers you a contract: you must die to your old self, and He will give you new life. When you were living a wholly material existence in the world and pursuing its pleasures, you bore the likeness of the man of dust. Now you are asked to renounce the world and to put on the likeness of the man from heaven. Just as in the past you yielded your bodies to impurity and greed as slaves of sin, now yield them to holiness as servants of God.

God is calling you to be disciples of the New Covenant, and to be renewed in heart and spirit. All the citizens of heaven look forward to the day when you will enter into the mysteries of Christ. The Gospel tells us that there is joy in heaven over the repentance of one sinner (see Luke 15:7). If that is so, what celebrations there will be over the saving of all of you! So if any of you are burdened with sin and bound by the chains of selfish habits, listen to the word of the Lord speaking in prophecy through Isaiah: "Wash yourselves, make yourselves clean, put all your evil practices out of My sight" (Is. 1:16). When you do that, all the angels will rejoice over you, and a great shout will go up: "Blessed are those whose disobedience is forgiven, and whose sins are blotted out!" (Ps. 32:1).

Take My yoke upon you

Jesus tells us that if we want to experience His rest, we must take up His yoke and learn from Him. Taking up His yoke means forgetting the past, guarding our eyes and tongues, controlling our passions, and establishing our souls in peace. It means refusing admittance to anger, resentment, hatred, violence, unlawful desires, or self-indulgence. Saint Paul says that when self-indulgence dominates us, the results are immorality, indecency, sexual irresponsibility, idolatry, witchcraft, feuds, quarrels, jealousy, ill-temper, cliques, envy, drunkenness, and debauchery. But when we are led by the Spirit, the harvest is very different:

love, joy, peace, patience, kindness, goodness, loyalty, gentleness, and self-control (Gal. 5:19–23). These are the fruits we must strive to bring forth. Not that we can produce anything of ourselves; but if we do what we can to root out all our vices and purify our hearts, we shall be ready to receive the grace of God in all its fullness and to preserve the blessings He gives us.

Now is the acceptable time

This is the Lenten season, the time for putting away sin and turning to the Lord in repentance. Confess your past sins—the deceitful, angry, boastful, or hurtful words; the selfish, dishonest, or immoral actions; the sins of the heart and the sins of the soul; the sins committed at night and the sins committed during the day. The Lord says to us in the Scriptures: "At the acceptable time I will listen to you" (2 Cor. 6:2). Now is the acceptable time. Renounce your sins, and you will receive the seal of the Holy Spirit "on the day of salvation"—that is, on the day of your baptism.

Yield your heart like wax to the impression of this seal; remove from it every worldly preoccupation. You are leaving the things of the world behind you. These things are unimportant; the gift of the Holy Spirit is the real treasure. So set your hope on what is to come. May the Lord Jesus Himself, our great High Priest, accept your lives as you lay them before Him and present you all to His Father as a gift offering, saying: "Here I am, with the children You have given Me" (Heb. 2:13). And may the Father keep you all in His love for ever. Amen.

Chapter Three

God made us free to choose

We were talking last time about the new life God offers us, and the response we must make to His invitation. Today I must say a few more words on the subject of sin.

When I talk about sin, I am speaking of matters involving a person's deliberate choice. God has made us free to choose right or wrong. He says through the Prophet Jeremiah: "I planted you as a good vine, sprung from sound seed. How is it that you have turned into a degenerate wild vine?" (Jer. 2:2). This gives us a picture of a good tree that deliberately chooses to bear bad fruit. It is not the fault of the gardener who planted the tree, intending that it should bear good fruit. It has freely chosen to bear bad fruit, so it will have to be burned. Another thing Scripture says is that God made men and women upright, but they have pursued devious ways (Eccl. 7:29). We are God's handiwork; He made us to do good works (Eph. 2:10). The good God could not make evil creatures; it is they who turn to evil of their own free will.

Now what causes us to make this choice for evil? It is not something outside ourselves, something upon which we could cast the blame. No, it is an evil weed that we allow to spring up in our own hearts; we let it grow instead of rooting it out. Scripture says: "Let your eyes look straight ahead of you" (Prov. 4:25), because if your eye does not wander you will not be tempted to lust or covetousness. Bear God's judgment in mind, and no sin will get the better of you. It is when you forget God that you begin to think sinful thoughts and commit sinful actions.

No one can force you to do wrong

Yet you are not on your own in this. You have a partner who prompts you—the devil.

The devil is the father of lies. He was a sinner and murderer from the start. That is the Lord's statement, not mine (1 John 3:8). No one sinned before the devil did. It was not because he had been created with sinful tendencies he could not help. If that had been so, the responsibility for his fall would belong to the one who made him. No, he was created good. He was actually an archangel who became a devil of his own choice and acquired the name Satan, which means Adversary and Slanderer. When he fell from grace he dragged down many other angels with him. His whole ambition now is to win over as many free men and women as possible to join him in rebelling against God. This is why he tempts anyone willing to listen to him. He is the author of adultery, murder, theft, vainglory, lying, and every kind of evil. It was through listening to him that our first parents were turned out of Paradise.

However, the devil can only make suggestions; he cannot force you to do wrong. Do not let him persuade you. If you shut the door and refuse to listen to him, he will not be able to hurt you. It is only when you allow sinful suggestions to enter your mind that they will strike root in your heart through your imagination. They will then take you captive and drag you down into a morass of evil.

Maybe you think your faith is strong enough for you to

entertain temptations without coming to any harm. You think you can handle any situation without danger. Let me tell you that a tiny root growing in the fissure of a rock can split that rock apart. In the same way the seed of sin can destroy your faith. Pull it up by the roots straight away. If you give it a chance to grow and get a firm hold, you will have to take an axe to it later on. It may even have to be burned out by fire.

There is only one unforgivable sin

Alas, you say, we have already sinned! Surely we have no hope of salvation now that we have been led astray? We have fallen; we can never stand up again. We have been blinded; we shall never see the light any more. We are cripples; we cannot hope to jump up and walk. We are dead; we can never rise again.

Do not despair. Lazarus had been dead four days and corruption had already set in when the Lord Jesus called him back to life. Can He not raise you up just as easily? There is only one unforgivable sin, and that is to refuse to believe that God will forgive you. All you need is the will to be saved, and faith in the Lord's power. This power is yours for the asking, so long as you do not count on your own strength but upon God's loving help.

Those who have been catechumens for a long time and have heard the scripture readings week by week in the liturgy need no proof of God's love for His people. But for those of you who have only recently come to Christianity, I will give a few instances from the Old Testament. There were times when the whole people of Israel sinned as one man, yet God did not stop loving them. They made a golden calf and worshipped it, but the Lord did not abandon them. They denied their God, but He did not deny His own goodness. Though they danced round the golden calf chanting, "These are your gods, Israel!" He saved them.

Even the high priest Aaron sinned along with the people.

But Moses prayed for him and the Lord forgave him. Now if Moses obtained pardon for a sinful priest, will not God's only Son Jesus obtain pardon for you? God did not forbid Aaron to continue in the high priest's office on account of his lapse; has He forbidden you to come for the grace of baptism because you used to be a pagan? Repent as Aaron did, and you will not be refused grace. From now on live an honest and clean life in God's sight, and you will find Him a truly loving Father.

David gives us another example of repentance. Though he was a man after God's own heart, he still fell into grave sin. He gave way to lust and committed adultery, then tried to escape responsibility by sending an innocent man to his death. But the Lord sent the Prophet Nathan to accuse him and bring him to repentance. Though David was a king, he did not take it amiss that a subject of his should speak so boldly. Since he knew Nathan to be the Lord's messenger, his immediate reaction was to exclaim: "I have sinned against the Lord." Mark this royal example of humility and confession. David fully admitted his evil action, and the Lord swiftly healed him. We know this because Nathan replied at once: "The Lord has taken away your sin" (2 Sam. 12:7–15). Even so, the king did penance. He accepted God's forgiveness, but he still fasted and put on sackcloth and shed tears.

Think too how Saint Peter, the leader of the Apostles, denied his Master three times out of fear of a serving-maid. Yet when Peter repented and wept bitterly, Jesus forgave him and even confirmed him in his appointment as head of His Church.

There are many other examples in the Bible of people who sinned, but afterward repented and were saved. We shall be reminded of them again during these weeks of Lent as we listen to the readings, and your catechists will go through them all with you. The Lord is full of love and kindness; He delights in forgiving and is very slow to punish us. So turn to Him with all your heart, and you will receive forgiveness for all the sins of your past life. You will be counted worthy to be born again and to inherit the Kingdom of heaven with all the saints, because from now on you will belong to Jesus Christ, the Lord of glory.

Chapter Four

The law of sin and death

In our last session, I talked about God's desire to forgive our sins and give us new life. Today, I want to explain the way in which He made our forgiveness possible through the death and Resurrection of our Lord Jesus Christ.

In the beginning the Lord created man out of dust. He made Adam and Eve immortal, fashioning them in His own image and likeness and showering gifts upon them. He gave them the beautiful garden of Paradise to be their home, and put the whole of creation under Adam's authority. There was one condition only, a simple test of obedience: Adam and Eve were allowed to eat the fruit of all the trees in the garden except one.

Alas, they did not fulfill the condition. Eve listened to the seductive voice of the serpent, and Adam listened to the persuasions of his wife. If only they had exercised discernment and remained loyal to their benefactor! Instead they played into the hands of the devil, who envied them the home in Paradise from which he himself had been expelled, and devised a scheme to rob them of the honor God had given to mankind. The devil tempted the man and the woman to covet the prerogatives and the glory of God Himself. He led them on to the ambition of becoming equal to and independent of their Maker and of deciding for themselves what was right and what was wrong. They succumbed to the devil's suggestions and fell into sin. In consequence they lost the promise of immortality and became subject to death. The Lord passed sentence on them. "You are dust," He declared, "and to dust you shall return" (Gen. 3:19).

Death was to be the inescapable lot of every man and woman coming into the world. No longer were Adam and Eve permitted to live in Paradise. God condemned them to sweat, toil, and pain as constant reminders of their disobedience and weakness. They now experienced the frailty of the human condition. Death and corruption had entered the world through sin, and had so weakened their nature that they became more and more liable to fall. Thus sin and death increased in mutual proportion. Even the laws God gave mankind for the amendment of sin led to their multiplication, and those who broke these laws by sinning drew down punishment upon themselves. And all the time the devil's bitter zeal against the human race intensified, because the sight of our corruption and ruin added to his triumph and glee.

The divine solution

But God still loved the world He had made, and He wanted His original blessing upon it to endure. In spite of Adam's rejection of his Maker, the Lord did not reject the human race. Though He condemned Adam and Eve to suffering and death in punishment of their sin, He used that same suffering and death as a remedy also. He determined to bring the devil's machinations to nothing and to banish his evil tyranny from the earth.

However, the divine condemnation could not be abolished by purely human means. The solution had to come from God. In His infinite wisdom and mercy, the remedy God conceived was this: human beings should indeed die as they deserved, but they should rise again to new life. In this way death, which was to be the instrument of their punishment, would also become the instrument of their everlasting happiness. God made death the doorway to immortality, thereby demonstrating His loving care for His children and exposing the folly of the devil's devices. Satan threw us out of Paradise, but the Lord gave us entry into heaven. The profit was greater than the penalty.

Jesus has restored our freedom

So then, by means of man's death the divine sentence was satisfied. Created immortal on condition of his abstaining from sin, man became mortal as a result of his disobedience. But to ensure that God's goodness to the human race should not be cut off by death, the Lord found a way to restore the heavenly blessing which the whole race had lost through the serpent's deceit.

He decided to become man Himself. The Father sent His only Son Jesus Christ into the world to share our human nature, to be born of Adam's stock and to live among us. In this way God raised up for Himself a Man who would keep the divine law perfectly. Left to ourselves, none of us could do this, because in our fallen condition we lacked the power to overcome the weakness of the flesh and the temptations of the evil one. By showing Himself to be free of all sin, Jesus proved that He was exempt from the death sentence. Yet in spite of the fact that Jesus had done nothing worthy of death, the devil used his own servants among men to bring an unjust death upon Him. Jesus did not resist; He accepted death at the hands of His enemies, appealing to His Father's justice for vindication.

Since the death sentence had been passed upon Him unjustly and wickedly, His Father released Him from it and raised Him to life again. Now He could no longer die; from that time on His Body was immune to death. Immortal and imperishable, He ascended to heaven high above the reach of Satan's malice. It was impossible for Satan to do any more harm to a man who was no longer subject to death or decay, a man who was impervious to his assaults and was living in perfect union with God in heaven. A member of our own race now had freedom of access to God. Accordingly God made Him legate for the whole of mankind, in order that the rest of us should share in this wonderful transformation. This is what Saint Paul means when he says to the Romans: "Who shall bring any charge against God's chosen ones? It is God who justifies us; who can condemn us? Christ has died and risen again, and now intercedes for us at the right hand of God" (Rom. 8:33, 34). No one can alter our right to this blessing. Since Christ died and rose again for us and is now with God the Father in heaven, He is able through His intercession to bring us to share His risen life and glory.

We enter into freedom through baptism

However, we still have to live out our lives on this earth. It was to prevent the deceit and snares of the devil from gaining control of men and women during their mortal lives that baptism was devised. Through the sacramental sign of baptism, we are delivered from the curse and enter into the freedom which the Lord Jesus gained for us; we obtain a share in the new and wonderful life of which He is the source. We now look forward to enjoying supernatural gifts which we could never have dreamed of possessing. No eye has seen nor ear heard, nor has human imagination conceived the wonderful things God has prepared for those who love Him (1 Cor. 2:9).

At present you do not yet experience the joy that is ahead of you. You are still in exile; tears are your bread by night and by day. People say to you, "Where is your God?" and you are unable to show them, because it is impossible to describe to people living on the level of the senses the things God has in store for those who trust in Him.

But do not be discouraged; the day will come when you will enter into the Lord's presence. He will come Himself and fulfill the promises which He has freely made. Nothing has been changed; He has not gone back on His word. He has put Himself under an obligation toward us, even though we are the ones who owe Him everything. He owed no one anything, because He is totally free of sin; yet when He found us oppressed by a terrible burden of condemnation, He had pity on us and set us free from the debt of everlasting punishment. From oppression and violence He redeems everyone who believes in Him, everyone who says to Him with all his heart: "I believe I shall see the Lord's goodness in the land of the living" (Ps. 27:13).[5]

Chapter Five

God has revealed hidden mysteries through His Son

Human minds and human words are altogether unequal to the grandeur of the things I have to talk to you about. No language is really capable of explaining the sacred mysteries of our religion. It is not easy even to give an exact description of created things, because their Maker has fashioned them with an infinite wisdom. But the things I have to tell you about during the coming weeks are things far above our finite human nature, things that cannot be encompassed by the human mind. They defeat all our efforts to put them into adequate words.

And yet the Great and Holy Feast of Easter is at hand, when we shall be celebrating all these mysteries, and it is my duty to prepare you for it.

I am reassured by the thought that from the beginning, before the world was made, it was the Father's will to reveal His hidden wisdom through His Son Jesus Christ. Through His Son He has made His secrets known to us and shown us gifts of incomparable splendor, giving human beings knowledge of these things through His Holy Spirit. Yes, Scripture says that God has revealed these things to us by His Spirit and has shown us glorious mysteries beyond all description (1 Cor. 2:10), mysteries which have been accomplished by the Spirit's power, by means of which we become capable through faith of raising ourselves up and taking hold of the things He has in store for us. So I have confidence that God will give me the grace to speak to you of these things which are so high above our natural human understanding, and enable me to fulfill my charge of instructing all who seek the grace of baptism at the Easter solemnity.

The old order is superseded

In Jesus Christ the old order of things is superseded and a whole new way of life is revealed. Scripture says that everyone who is in Christ is a new creature: the old order has passed away and all is made new (2 Cor. 5:17). Death and decay are ended; we are no longer subject to the tyranny of our passions and our human inconstancy.

The life of the new creation is already present. We shall know this life in all its fullness at the resurrection of the dead; on that day, by the power of God, we who are old and toil-worn will become young and vigorous, we who are subject to death and decay will become immortal and imperishable. This is the new covenant the Lord has made with us, and this is His promise to all who are renewed and born again.

God gives us the sacraments as a guarantee

To believe in these blessings which are still hidden from us in the future we need a very strong faith. We might find it hard to believe that such greatness could ever be ours if God had not given us the sacraments as a guarantee. In the sacraments, by means of signs and figures, we are able here and now to lay hold of the things we hope to possess in the future, and with an unwavering faith that these things are already ours, we are given the power to live a life worthy of that new world. As far as is possible here below, we base our life in this world on the word of

Scripture that says: "We are citizens of heaven and our home is with God, with whom we have a permanent dwelling place not of human fabrication" (2 Cor. 5:1). By virtue of our baptism, our names are already inscribed on the list of those who are to be glorified in the world to come. So even while we are still on earth we try to practice a heavenly way of life as far as we possibly can; we try to detach our hearts from transitory things and to fix them on what is to come.

You must realize that everyone who approaches these holy sacraments has been called by God's grace, otherwise he would be unable to aspire to something so far above the power of human nature. What we receive in baptism is not some ordinary, commonplace gift, but the gift of becoming an entirely new creature and of acquiring every kind of spiritual blessing and virtue, through the life of divine grace which we receive. In our natural state we are weak creatures, fickle and changeable, subject to pain and distress, and continually falling back into the nothingness from which we came. By the gift of God we are going to become immortal, incorruptible, unchangeable, and immune to suffering. From slaves we shall be changed into free men and women, from enemies of God into friends, from outsiders into sons and daughters. We shall no longer be counted as members of the race of Adam, but as members of Christ; we shall have Christ, not Adam, as our head, because it will be Christ's life that we live. No longer shall we labor to cultivate an earth that brings forth nothing but brambles and thistles; we shall be citizens of heaven, far removed from every kind of sorrow and distress. Death will not reign over us any more; rather we ourselves shall reign in a new life, not as slaves of sin, but as servants of holiness, no longer in Satan's employ but at home with Jesus Christ and His Father for ever and ever.

Our hope must be unshakable

Our Lord said to Nicodemus: "Unless a man is born of water and the Spirit, he cannot enter the kingdom of heaven" (John 3:5). When we are reborn in baptism our names are immediately written in heaven and we become heirs to the good things to come. The full fruition of our new life will be given us in heaven, where Jesus has entered before us, and all who have believed in Him await the day of resurrection when they will make their home there with Him for ever. In the meantime their names are truly inscribed on the rolls of the heavenly city by means of these sacraments, just as they are inscribed in the register of the Church here on earth.

At the present time we need great earnestness of purpose and perseverance if we are not to fall away from our hope in this magnificent promise and find ourselves shut out of Paradise as Adam and Eve were. It is by making a strong and resolute profession of faith, without wavering, that we enter into these sacred mysteries, a profession which we must keep forever in our minds, taking every care to preserve the gift we receive. Although these heavenly blessings are already ours by faith, it is only after we have received them in their fullness and actually taken possession of our inheritance that there will be no further possibility of losing them. In this world below it is still possible for us to fall away, because our nature is changeable and weak. We must therefore be always on our guard, and make sure that our hope in God's promises is unshakable.

Lord, You are the helper of all;
it is You who set us free,
who save us and protect us.
Your strong arm has redeemed us
and all our hope is in You.
You have conquered sin and death;
through Your only Son You have brought Satan to nothing.
You have frustrated his tricks
and released the prisoners he kept in chains.
We bless and thank You for calling these catechumens to
    Yourself
through Your only Son,
and inviting them to Your holy mysteries.
Lord, strengthen their faith,
so that they may come to know You,
the only true God,
and Jesus Christ whom You have sent.
Help them to persevere with undivided attention
in learning all that You have to teach them.
May they progress day by day
until they are fit for the washing that will give them new
    birth
and are ready to receive Your holy mysteries.
We ask this through Your only Son, Jesus Christ,
in the Holy Spirit.
Through Him may all glory and power be Yours
for ever and ever.
Amen.[6]

III
THE CREED: SUMMARY OF THE CHRISTIAN FAITH

Chapter Six

Learn to see with the eyes of the spirit

As I have already said, all of you whose names have been written in the Church's sacred register must bring with you a generous faith and a strong resolution. Faith is essential for what is about to be accomplished among us here, because you need spiritual insight to understand these sacred mysteries. Faith will give you new eyes, eyes that are capable of perceiving what is invisible to the senses. Our bodily eyes can only see the objects which come into their range of vision, but the eyes of faith do not stop short at material things. It is characteristic of faith to attach itself to what is unseen as if it were clearly visible. Faith, Scripture tells us, gives substance to the things we hope for and makes us certain of things we do not yet see (Heb. 11:1).

So what I ask you to do now is to disregard outward appearances and learn to see with the eyes of the spirit. When you see the baptismal font, do not believe its contents are mere water; do not believe that the hand laid upon your head is only the bishop's. What happens in the sacraments is not the work of mortal men but of God's Holy Spirit. It is the Spirit who sanctifies the water, and the Spirit who comes down upon you as the bishop lays his hand on your head.

Faith has a twofold meaning

There is one word for faith in our language, but it has two meanings. There is the faith that has to do with doctrines and involves an intellectual assent; and there is the faith that trusts so completely in the promises of God that it empowers activities impossible to unaided human nature. Without the first kind we could not have the second, because unless we have a sound belief in God and in the Incarnation and redeeming work of Jesus Christ, we shall not be able to trust our Savior absolutely.

Of the first kind of faith the Lord Jesus said: "Whoever hears My words and believes in the one who sent Me has everlasting life, and he will not be condemned" (John 5:24). If you believe that Jesus Christ is Lord and that God raised Him from the dead, you will be saved and admitted to heaven by Him, just as the good thief was led by Him into Paradise. I assure you that this is true. Jesus saved the good thief for one brief and genuine act of faith, and if you believe in Him He will save you too with equal power.

The second kind of faith is given by a special grace. It is the kind of faith Saint Paul speaks of when he says: "To one person the Spirit gives the word of wisdom, to another the word of knowledge, to another faith, to another gifts of healing" (1 Cor. 12:8, 9). Anyone who has this kind of faith can say to a mountain, "Move yourself and go over there," and the mountain will move. When someone can give a command like that, believing that it will happen and without any secret doubts, then he has indeed received the charismatic gift of faith. Jesus likened this kind of faith to a grain of mustard seed. A grain of mustard seed is small, but it contains an explosive energy; it can be planted in a tiny space, and then sends out great branches all round, so that when it is fully grown it can give shelter to the birds. In the same way the faith the Spirit gives us achieves tremendous things by one brief, swift decision.

The faith we profess at our baptism

But for the moment let us think of the faith we profess when we make our commitment to Jesus Christ at our baptism.

By this faith we know that there is one God, the source of all things, who made everything out of nothing. By this faith we know that the dead will rise again. By faith we know that the Father has a Son who shares His own nature. By faith we know that the Holy Spirit is God and that He is the Spirit of Father and Son. By faith we are convinced of the truth of the saving plan by which God the Son became incarnate in our world.

Faith makes us grasp with our hearts things that do not yet actually exist. What I mean is that by faith we firmly lay hold of the resurrection and the Kingdom of heaven and the life to come, which we do not actually experience here and now. Faith makes us see and know invisible and inexpressible realities. By faith we are able to see God, who is by nature invisible, who dwells in unapproachable light and glory, which no human eyes have ever seen or can see (1 Tim. 6:16). Yes, we are able to see this glory with the eyes of faith! Just as we can see material things as long as our bodily eyes are healthy and have good vision and remain unobstructed, so through the teaching of our religion we come to know these invisible and inexpressible things. We can see them correctly if our faith is sound, but they are invisible to people whose faith is infirm. Faith gives a perfect grasp of religious truth to those it convinces, but those who fall away from faith are plunged into error. Saint Paul calls the Church of God the pillars and bulwark of the truth (1 Tim. 3:15), because it is sound in faith and strong in teaching.

Now the faith the Church commits to you is confirmed by God's word in the Scriptures. Not everyone, however, can study the Bible and know it thoroughly. Some lack the education, others the opportunity. For this reason, we are given a summary of the whole teaching of the Christian faith in a short formula, easy to remember, so that no one will be lost through not learning it.

The Creed

We call this formula the Creed. It consists of twelve brief articles which have been collected from the Scriptures and drawn up in a way people can easily memorize.

The time has now come for me to teach it to you. I want you to commit it to memory word for word. Do not write it down on paper; write it in your hearts so that you never forget it. Say it over every day among yourselves. Before you go to sleep at night, before you go out of your house during the day, fortify yourselves with the Creed. And as I explain it to you, believe it, and be ready to recite it publicly next week.

The Creed is part of your Christian armor. It is a provision for your journey that you must retain as long as your life lasts. Never accept any other faith than this, not even if I should change my mind and say something that contradicts what you are now being taught; no, not if the spirit of darkness were to disguise himself as an angel of light and lead you astray. Guard it with the utmost care, or the old enemy will seize his chance to ruin you by tempting you to prefer your own notions to the teaching of the Church, or else some false Christian will deceive you by misrepresenting the truths that have been handed on to you. Faith, you might say, is like cash paid over the counter. I am handing over the cash to you now, but God will require an account from you of what you have received. Remember what Saint Paul says to Timothy: "I charge you before God, who gives life to all, and before Jesus Christ who gave testimony before Pontius Pilate, to keep this faith that is committed to you spotless until our Lord Jesus Christ appears. A treasure of life has been entrusted to you, and at His coming the Master will look for the deposit" (1 Tim. 5:21; 6:13–15).

Chapter Seven

The Giving of the Creed

I hope that after our last session you are all prepared this morning for me to hand over the Creed to you.

The Creed is the formula by which we profess the Christian faith. By publicly affirming these few short phrases at baptism we gain immense blessings. The Creed is also the rule of faith by which we are able to judge the orthodoxy of any doctrine we may hear propounded. If a proposition cannot be reconciled with these basic tenets, it must be rejected.

First of all, I will recite the Creed straight through for you. Listen carefully.

I BELIEVE IN GOD THE FATHER ALMIGHTY,
MAKER OF HEAVEN AND EARTH,
AND IN JESUS CHRIST, HIS ONLY SON, OUR LORD,
WHO WAS CONCEIVED OF THE HOLY SPIRIT
AND BORN OF THE VIRGIN MARY,
SUFFERED UNDER PONTIUS PILATE,
WAS CRUCIFIED, DIED, AND WAS BURIED.
ON THE THIRD DAY HE ROSE FROM THE DEAD.
HE ASCENDED INTO HEAVEN

AND IS SEATED AT THE RIGHT HAND OF THE FATHER.
FROM THENCE HE SHALL COME
TO JUDGE THE LIVING AND THE DEAD.
I BELIEVE IN THE HOLY SPIRIT,
THE HOLY CATHOLIC CHURCH,
THE FORGIVENESS OF SINS,
THE RESURRECTION OF THE BODY,
AND LIFE EVERLASTING.
AMEN.[7]

Now let us consider each article of the Creed separately.

God the Father

The first article is:

I BELIEVE IN GOD THE FATHER ALMIGHTY.

How quickly I can say this, and yet how packed with truth it is! It tells us that God is both God and Father; a God of all power, and a Father of all goodness. How wonderful to discover that our Lord and Master is also our Father! Believe in God your Father, and be assured of receiving all you need from His loving kindness, because He is almighty. To be sure, this is not your first discovery that God is almighty. But you will begin to experience Him as your Father when Mother Church has given you new birth in baptism. As catechumens you were conceived in the Church's womb; when you are born again as children of God you will be able to cry out: "Abba, Father!"

So then, we believe in God the Father almighty. Let none of you say: "God can never forgive my sins. I have done such terrible things." Can the almighty God not do anything He pleases? You think you have committed such sins that it is impossible for you ever to be clean again and set free. I tell you God is almighty.

Do we not sing in the psalms: "Bless the Lord, my soul, and never forget all His blessings. He has forgiven all your sins and healed every one of your ills" (Ps. 103:2, 3)? It is precisely because of our great misery that we need God's almighty power.

Now God the Father almighty is

MAKER OF HEAVEN AND EARTH.

He has the power to make whatever He chooses; He makes heaven and earth, immortal souls and mortal bodies, all things visible and invisible. Yes, in His almighty power He is able to do whatever He pleases. Nevertheless, there are some things He cannot do. He cannot die, He cannot sin, He cannot lie, He cannot deceive. These things He is unable to do; if He could do them, He would not be almighty. Our almighty Father is absolutely incapable of sinning. He does whatever He likes; this is what we mean by being almighty. Yes, He does every good and right thing that He chooses to do; as for what is evil, He does not choose to do it. Believe in Him then, and confess His name. By believing in our hearts we are put right with God, but by confessing with our lips we are saved, says Saint Paul (Rom. 10:10). You must believe in your hearts and, when the time comes for you to recite the Creed you have learned, you must also confess with your lips. So receive the Creed now, make it your own, and afterward render it back. Never forget it.

Belief in God's almighty power means believing that there is no creature whatever that He has not made. He did not, of course, make sin. Sin has no real being. It is rather the corruption of His creation, and that is why He punishes it. You must not doubt God's almighty power on account of those who disobey His will, because when people do what God does not wish, He turns the evil they do into the good He does wish. Nothing can overcome His will or change it; whether we are justly condemned or mercifully saved, the will of almighty God is done. The only thing God cannot do is what He does not want to do. He uses evil people, not according to their depravity but according to His goodness, for He made these people good and He can turn their evil actions into good. If He did not know how to bring good out of evil, He would never have allowed those people to be born. We cannot find words to express the good that has come about through our Savior's Passion and through His blood that was poured out for the forgiveness of our sins; yet this immense good came through the malice of Satan, the envy of men, and the treachery of Judas.

God the Son

Very well, then. What comes next?

AND IN JESUS CHRIST, HIS ONLY SON, OUR LORD.

Now if Jesus Christ is the Son of God the Father almighty, then He is God the Father's equal. If He is the Father's only Son, then He shares His Father's almighty power and His eternal being. God's only Son must be God, otherwise He would not be a true son. Think of earthly creatures: whatever their kind, that they reproduce. Human beings do not give birth to oxen, nor birds to dogs, nor dogs to sheep. The nature of the offspring is the nature of the sire. Mortal creatures bring forth mortal offspring. The immortal God begets an only Son of the same immortal nature as Himself. The Son is almighty as His Father is. Father and Son have one single will. The Father is God, the Son is God; both are one single God. Some people think God the Father is greater than God the Son. That would mean there were two gods. Do not countenance such a suggestion. If you believe that, you have set up an idol in your heart. Throw it down at once!

Believe first, then you will understand. When God gives the gift of faith, understanding follows. So if you cannot yet understand, make an act of faith.

God became man

Now let us see what the only Son of God the Father almighty has done for us, and what He suffered on our behalf.

HE WAS CONCEIVED OF THE HOLY SPIRIT
AND BORN OF THE VIRGIN MARY.

He who is the great God, equal to the Father, humbled Himself and was born of a woman in order to heal our pride. Man was puffed up with pride, and down he fell. God humbled Himself, and raised him up. He stretched out His hand to us as we lay in the dust. We stumbled and fell; He came down from heaven to rescue us. We lay in the dust; He stooped down to us. Let us take the hand He stretches out to us and rise to our feet, so as not to fall into everlasting torment.

He came to us through the Virgin Mary; His conception was brought about by the Holy Spirit, not by Mary's husband. In this way the Son of God put on our human flesh; in this way our Maker became one of us. He assumed a nature not His own, without giving up the nature that was His. The Word was made flesh and dwelt among us. The invisible God made Himself visible, and lived with men and women on earth. The only Son of the Father became one of the human race. He is our only Savior; we have no other. He has redeemed us, not with gold or silver, but with His own precious blood.

He redeemed us

Now let us look at the way He redeemed us.

HE SUFFERED UNDER PONTIUS PILATE,
WAS CRUCIFIED,
DIED, AND WAS BURIED.

Astounding thought! Who was it that suffered? The only Son of God, our Lord! What did He suffer? Crucifixion, death, and burial! For whom? For sinners and criminals.

What amazing condescension, what depths of loving mercy! How can I ever repay the Lord for His goodness to me? He chose the most terrible death, so that those who bear witness to Him should not fear death of any kind.

He was the Lord, the only Son of the Father, yet He was crucified. It was in His human nature that He was crucified, and only His human body lay in the grave; yet we say that Jesus Christ our Lord, the only Son of the Father, was buried. The Man who was conceived of the Holy Spirit and born of the Virgin Mary was Jesus Christ our Lord, the Father's only Son. The Man who was crucified under Pontius Pilate was Jesus Christ our Lord, the Father's only Son. Only His body lay in the grave. But we must not despise this mere body; it was when His body lay in the grave that Christ redeemed us. Why do I say this? Because He did not lie there for ever.

ON THE THIRD DAY HE ROSE AGAIN FROM THE DEAD.

This is what the Creed tells us in the next article. When we profess our faith in the Lord's Passion, we go on to proclaim our faith in His Resurrection.

What did Jesus do when He suffered? He taught us endurance. And when He rose again? He showed us what to hope for. The one was the task, the other the reward.

But having risen from the dead, Jesus did not remain here below. Listen to the next article:

HE ASCENDED INTO HEAVEN.

And where is He now?

HE IS SEATED AT THE RIGHT HAND OF THE FATHER.

Believe this. When I say He is seated, understand that He is with His Father in heaven, just as sometimes we speak of a person's country seat, meaning his home. We don't mean the owner sits there perpetually and never gets up and walks about. So when you are asked to believe that Jesus Christ sits at the Father's right hand, it simply means that He is there with the Father, sharing His joy. And when I say the right hand, don't start looking for a left hand. By the right hand of the Father is meant eternal happiness: inexpressible, immeasurable, unimaginable joy and blessedness. There Jesus, our brother, has His home.

He will come again
What next?

FROM THENCE HE SHALL COME
TO JUDGE THE LIVING AND THE DEAD.

That is, He will judge those who are still alive at His Second Coming, together with the dead who have already gone to the grave before them.

We can also understand the living as people who are spiritually alive, and the dead as people who are dead in their sins. Christ will judge both kinds, giving each his due. To those who have done good He will say: "Come, blessed of My Father, enter into your inheritance. Receive the Kingdom that has been prepared for you from the beginning of the world."

My brothers and sisters, let this be your ambition. Do all

you can to be ready for this one thing, to have the joy of hearing these words addressed to you: "Come, blessed of My Father, enter into your inheritance, receive the Kingdom prepared for you." For to those who have not done good Christ will say: "Go away from Me, you cursed, into the unending fire prepared for the devil and his servants" (Matt. 25:34, 41.)

This is how Jesus Christ will judge the living and the dead. I urge you to accept Him now as your Savior, and then you will not need to be afraid of Him as your Judge. Whoever believes in Him now and keeps His commandments and loves Him will not be afraid when He comes to judge the living and the dead; on the contrary, he will long for His coming. What could make us happier than the coming of someone we love and long for?

Still, we must not be careless. We must have a certain fear, because He will be our Judge. Saint John tells us that if we say we have not committed any sins, we deceive ourselves and there is no truth in us; but if we confess our sins, God is faithful and just. He will forgive our sins and cleanse us from all wrong-doing. "I have written this to you," says Saint John, "to keep you from sinning. But if anyone does commit sin, we have an advocate with the Father, Jesus Christ the Just One; He is the propitiation for our sins" (1 John 2:1, 2).

What joy that the one who is to be our future judge is already our advocate! Even now He is interceding for us at the right hand of the Father. If we have Him as our advocate, shall we fear Him as our Judge? No! We have sent Him on ahead of us to plead our cause, and so we look forward in confidence to His return.

We have now dealt with the articles of the Creed that tell us about God the Father's almighty power and goodness, and those that tell us about Jesus Christ, His only Son, our Lord. We have spoken of the Son's birth from all eternity, and of His birth from a virgin in the fullness of time; of how He did not cling to

His equality with God, but emptied Himself, not by giving up His divinity but by taking the nature of a slave (see Phil. 2:7), and how by means of our human nature the invisible God became visible, the almighty became weak, the immortal one died; how in our human nature He rose from the dead and ascended into heaven (which as God He had never left), and how He is now seated at the right hand of the Father.

God the Holy Spirit

It is through Him that the Holy Spirit has been sent to us from the Father. The Holy Spirit is equal to the Father and the Son in all things. When we say:

I BELIEVE IN THE HOLY SPIRIT

we are completing our profession of faith in that most blessed Trinity of Persons which is one single God, all-powerful, invisible, immortal, ruler of the ages, Creator of all things seen and unseen. He is the God of Abraham, Isaac, and Jacob, the author of the Old Testament and the author of the New, for there is one God the Father, the God of Old Testament and New. There is one Lord Jesus Christ, foretold in the prophecies of the Old Testament and present in the New. And there is one Holy Spirit, who through the Prophets proclaimed Christ's coming and then, when Christ did come, came down Himself in the form of a dove to make Him known.

These three are not three gods, but one. This is a difficult teaching for human minds to grasp. We have to believe it in order to understand it. Unless you believe, says the Prophet Isaiah, you will never come to any understanding (Is. 7:9). Believe then in the Holy Spirit; believe that He is God, that it was by His power that Jesus was born of a virgin and rose from the dead, that it was by His power that the Apostles worked signs and wonders, and that by His power believers are born to new life in baptism.

If you want to experience the Holy Spirit's power, be baptized, and you will become His temple. "Do you not know," says Saint Paul, "that your bodies are a temple, the dwelling place of the Holy Spirit whom you have received from God?" (1 Cor. 6:19). You will know Him in the depths of your being as a fountain of living water springing up within you, calling out, "Come to the Father!"

Chapter Eight

The Church is your mother

So far we have professed our faith in the blessed Trinity—Father, Son, and Holy Spirit. The remaining articles of the Creed are about ourselves.

The next thing we say is:

I BELIEVE IN THE HOLY CATHOLIC CHURCH.

The Church is ourselves. Not just the people present here in this building listening to me speaking, but all who by God's grace hold the Christian faith, not only in this city but all over the world; all whom the Lord Jesus has redeemed with His precious blood and who profess their faith in this Creed which I am now teaching you.

This is how the Catholic Church understands herself. She is our true mother, because she is the Bride of Christ. He came down from heaven in search of her, and with infinite love and tenderness healed and cleansed her and showered His gifts upon her. She can never forget that once she prostituted herself to demons and false gods; to forget that would be to forget the mercy of her Savior, who found her a harlot and, by the power of His grace, restored her to virginity.

Yes, the Church is both virgin and mother; virgin by her faith and fidelity to her Lord, mother by the children she bears Him in the waters of baptism. Have you not given in your names to her in order to be born again? Are not all of you here at this moment being carried in her womb? Like Mary, the mother of Jesus, who bore her Son yet remained a virgin afterward, the Church preserves her virginity even though she bears many children. Like Mary, she gives birth to Christ, because all the baptized are members of Christ's Body. The true children of Holy Church resemble their mother; they too give birth to Christ, since He Himself said: "Whoever does the will of My Father in heaven is My brother and sister and mother" (Matt. 12:50). And they too are virgins, since Saint Paul says: "I have betrothed you as a chaste virgin to your one husband, Christ" (2 Cor. 11:2). Saint Paul also calls the Church our mother, the heavenly Jerusalem (Gal. 4:26), while the Book of Revelation calls her the Bride, the wife of the Lamb (Rev. 21:9).

So then, Holy Church is your mother, the heavenly Jerusalem, the holy city of God. Love this mother of yours, who bears you in her womb. Honor and acknowledge her. Anyone who refuses to have the Church as his mother cannot have God as his Father. She is the Church of the living God, the pillar and bulwark of the truth (1 Tim. 3:15), who does not reject sinners who come to take part in her sacraments, even though in the end they may be separated from her.

Do not be scandalized if you discover that there are sinners within the Church. They are the chaff among the wheat, and are allowed to remain until the final winnowing on the Last Day, in the hope that they may be touched by the Church's message of repentance and forgiveness in Jesus' name. To her the Lord has given the keys of the Kingdom of heaven, so that through her ministry and the power of the Spirit sins may be washed away in the blood of the Lamb. In this Holy Catholic Church we who used to lie dead in sin are born anew, to live the resurrection life with Christ, by whose grace we have all been saved.

The Church has the power to forgive sins

The Creed goes on to say:

I BELIEVE IN THE FORGIVENESS OF SINS.

If the Church did not possess the power of forgiving sins, there would be no hope for any of us, no hope of healing or freedom or of eternal life in our heavenly home. Thanks be to God for empowering His Church with this priceless gift! Here are all of you now, ready to come to the sacred font where you will be washed clean and made new creatures by being born again in the saving waters of baptism. When you come up from the font you will be free of every sin; all the guilt of your past will be blotted out. No matter what you have done, it will be forgiven. You can tell me the most terrible crime you have ever committed, so horrible that you shudder to think of it, but I shall say to you: even so, you have not murdered God's only Son. Could anything be worse than that? That was the crime committed by some of the Lord's own people; yet after they had handed Him over to be crucified, a great many of them came to believe in Him on the Day of Pentecost. When they turned to Him in repentance and were baptized, that fearful sin of theirs was forgiven.

Have a firm hope, then, that by believing, repenting, and being baptized you too will receive the forgiveness of all your sins and be born to new life.

After your baptism hold fast to your new life by keeping God's commandments, so that you preserve your baptismal grace to the end of your life. I do not say you will be able to live in future without committing any sins, because it is impossible in this world to avoid lesser sins entirely. But the Lord has given us a remedy for these lighter offenses, which I shall tell you about later on.

We shall rise again

The next article of the Creed is:

I BELIEVE IN THE RESURRECTION OF THE BODY.

This resurrection has already happened for our Lord Jesus Christ, and we believe it will happen for us too, because we are His members. Jesus Christ is the Head of the Church, which is His Body. Our Head has risen from the grave and gone before us to heaven. Where the head is, the members will follow.

The whole Christian mystery is the mystery of our resurrection. "If Christ has not risen," declares Saint Paul, "then your faith is in vain" (1 Cor. 15:14). But Christ *has* risen, and that is why our faith is so sure and certain.

How will our bodies rise again? Not in the way that Lazarus was brought back to life. He was raised up only for a time, and had to die again later on. We shall not come back to life in order to go on living the same kind of earthly life and pursuing the same earthly pleasures as we did before. Saint Paul makes that clear. He says our bodies will be sown in the ground as natural bodies, and raised up as spiritual bodies (1 Cor. 15:44). In the risen life our bodies will be fully under the control of our glorified spirits. They will no longer be a burden to us, nor will they have any need for food, since they will never suffer again or wear out. There will be no more death, no more sickness, no more hunger or thirst, no distress or old age or weariness. Our mortal bodies will put on immortality and imperishability. Body and spirit together will possess

LIFE EVERLASTING

—the next article of the Creed—and a common home with the angels in heaven. We shall be the Lord's possession and inheritance, and He will be ours.

This is the true, Christian, Catholic, and Apostolic Faith, based on the Lord's own words. Cast out every doubt, and believe firmly, totally, unswervingly. Trust the Lord, who cherishes every hair of your heads. For your sake He took a human body and soul so that He could die for you and rise again, and you might never again have any fear of death. How then can you hesitate to believe He is able to give you eternal life of body and soul?

The Holy Spirit will write the Creed in your hearts

Having given you this short teaching on the Creed, I have done my duty for the present. When you hear the Creed recited, you will recognize in it a brief summary of what I have just said. As for the actual words, as I told you at the beginning, you are strictly forbidden to write them down. You must learn them by heart.

You think that is impossible without putting them on paper? Not at all; you will remember them better if you do not write them down. When you write a thing down you know you can always read it again, so you do not take the trouble to go over it in your mind every day. But when you have not got it on paper you repeat it over and over again to make sure you do not forget it.

To know the Creed by heart is a great safeguard. There are bound to come times when you will be afflicted by dullness of spirit, weariness of body, temptations from the devil (who never takes a holiday), sickness, or anxiety of one kind or another. At such times you can find healing and strength in reaffirming your faith by repeating the words of the Creed.

Do not be afraid your memory will fail you. Everything you hear in the Creed is contained in Holy Scripture. You are hearing it all the time, not in its entirety or in the customary order, but as it occurs in the liturgy. Remember that God has promised through the Prophet Jeremiah that He will make a new covenant with us. "This is the covenant I will make with them in those days," He says. "I will write My laws in their minds and inscribe them in their hearts" (Jer. 31:33). As you hear the words of the Creed pronounced they are being written in your minds. But when you have been born again through the grace of the Lord Jesus who has called you to share His Kingdom and glory, the Holy Spirit will write them in your hearts, so that you will love your holy faith, and your faith will show itself by your love. Because of your love you will try to be pleasing to the Lord your God, the giver of all good things, not out of a servile fear of punishment, but by freely choosing to carry out His holy will and obey His commandments.

Chapter Nine

Preliminary rendering of the Creed

Brothers and sisters, we are more than halfway through Lent, and we still have many things to explain to you. Next Sunday marks an important stage in your preparation. It is the day when you will be asked one by one to recite the Creed in the presence of the bishop and all the faithful. In the meantime your sponsors and the kind families you are lodging with will go over the words with you and help you to memorize them.

No one need be anxious or nervous. The bishop is not a schoolmaster with a cane. You will simply be rehearsing your lesson to your father, not undergoing an examination. Even if one of you should trip up and make a mistake in the wording, it would not be a catastrophe. The important thing is not to fail in your faith. Then when the day comes for you to make your solemn commitment to Jesus Christ, you will again recite the Creed before the bishop as your profession of faith, and so you will be admitted to baptism and the Church of God, with full freedom of access to the heavenly city.

The meaning of the exorcisms

Next Sunday will be a milestone in your preparation for

another reason. It is the day when the most solemn of the exorcisms will be carried out. Unlike the daily exorcisms you have been patiently undergoing during these past weeks, next Sunday's exorcism will take place at a solemn public ceremony in church, with all the baptized there to support you.

This ceremony is called the Scrutiny. It is a kind of testing. It has indeed been a humiliating experience for you to have to stand each morning before the exorcist with bowed head, to feel his insulting breath on your face, and to hear curses hurled against the evil one who holds your spirit in bondage. But have courage; these exorcisms are no empty ritual. Their aim is to overcome the final assaults of the demon against you while you are still catechumens, and to prize you little by little from his iron grip. By means of the terrifying adjurations of the exorcist and the invocation of the name of the Lord Jesus, the devil's hold over you is gradually being weakened, for it is impossible for even the fiercest and most obstinate of demons not to depart in haste when he hears these alarming threats.

Soon you will be strong enough to renounce the evil one altogether. However, although your only outward part during the exorcisms is to submit to them in silence in an attitude of humility, inwardly you must be fully involved in the conflict. What we minister to you by calling on the name of your Redeemer, you must complete by searching your heart, repenting of your sins, and turning away from all wrongdoing. We counteract the assaults of the old enemy by our prayers to God and by rebuking the devil; it is up to you to persevere in prayer and repentance, so that you may deserve to be snatched from the powers of darkness and transferred to the Kingdom of God's holy light.

This is the task set before you now; this is what you must work at. While we hurl curses at the devil matching his own wickedness, you give battle too by renouncing your sins and turning away from him. His tyranny must be destroyed and conquered, because he is God's enemy as well as yours. By raging against God and plotting your destruction, he is adding to his own doom. But knowing himself accursed, he continues to breathe out fire and slaughter, to lay snares and to plot your ruin, to pour out his venom wherever he can.

Rid your hearts of all his poison by calling on the name of your Savior. Whatever horrible suggestions and unclean temptations he sends you, let them all come to the surface and be driven out. The time is very near for Satan to be despoiled of his slaves. That yoke of his that weighed you down in the past is going to be removed from your shoulders and put on Satan's own neck and on the necks of all his demons. All you have to do is give your free consent to your Redeemer for your deliverance.

Hope in Him, all you new people of His, the people who are being reborn, the people God is forming for Himself. Trust that you will be truly born again and healed, that you will not be stillborn, injured in the womb, aborted. See how Mother Church groans in labor to bring you to birth and into the light of faith! Do not injure your mother's womb by your impatient struggles, and so make your birth more painful and difficult. Praise your God, all you people whom He is creating, praise your Lord and Savior! He allows these delays before your birth so that you may be fully formed and ready. To Him it makes no difference whether the time is short or long, since He is eternal.

So I repeat: have courage. All these ordeals are nothing in comparison with the glory of the new life that awaits you. Be ready at cockcrow next Sunday, with your sponsors, and take your place before the bishop as your name is called out.

After the exorcism and your rendering of the Creed, we shall go on to teach you the meaning of Christian prayer.

Brothers and sisters, let us support our catechumens by praying more earnestly than ever that God will deliver them from all evil, from all sin, and from all diabolical assault; that He will prepare them for the waters of rebirth, for the forgiveness of sins, and for the garment of immortality; that He will bless their going out and their coming in throughout the whole of their lives, and bring all their labors to a happy conclusion.

And you yourselves, catechumens, ask the protection of the Spirit of peace. Pray that the blessing of peace may be poured out upon all you do, this day and every day of your life. Pray that you may so live as to die a holy Christian death, and so come into the presence of the living God and His Christ.[8]

Let us pray.
O Lord our God, we know that You are full of mercy and
    love toward the people You have made;
and so we come to You in humble confidence
to ask Your blessing on these servants of Yours
whom You have filled with the hope of being born anew by
    water and the Holy Spirit.
Give them Your peace and the true light of the Holy Spirit.
Number them among Your saints in heaven
and make them worthy of Your glorious Kingdom.
Bless and protect their going out and their coming in.
Deliver them from all evil and from all the attacks of the
    evil one,
and grant them forgiveness of all their sins.
Prepare them for the waters of rebirth,
and give them the garment of immortality.
We ask this through our Lord Jesus Christ, Your Son;
in His name we praise and bless and worship You, with the
    Holy Spirit, for ever and ever.
Amen.[9]

IV
THE SCRUTINY AND GIVING OF THE LORD'S PRAYER

The solemn exorcisms

The Scrutiny takes place in the church in the presence of all the clergy and faithful.

The candidates come forward for the exorcisms at the deacon's summons. Barefoot and dressed only in penitents' tunics, they stand on sackcloth with bowed heads, while the bishop prays:

God of Abraham, God of Isaac, and God of Jacob,
You are the God who appeared to Your servant Moses on
    Mount Sinai,
the God who led Israel out of Egypt.
In Your mercy You appointed an angel to guard them
day and night.
We ask You now, Lord,
to send Your holy angels to these servants of Yours also,
and bring them to the grace of baptism.

The deacon instructs their sponsors to make the sign of the cross on the foreheads of their respective godchildren. One of the exorcists then lays his hands on each of them in turn, saying in a loud voice:

Remember, you accursed devil,
the sentence that was passed upon you,

and give honor to the living and true God!
Give honor to Jesus Christ His Son,
and to the Holy Spirit,
and depart from these servants of God
whom our Lord Jesus Christ has called
to receive His holy grace and blessing
in the waters of baptism.
we adjure you, cursed devil,
never dare to violate it!

*An acolyte makes the sign of the cross on the foreheads of the
candidates. Then a second exorcist lays his hands on them, and
says:*

Hear this, you cursed devil!
I command you in the name of the eternal God
and of our Savior Jesus Christ
to depart in confusion,
a victim of your own envy.
You no longer have anything in common with these
      servants of God;
their thoughts are already turned toward heavenly things.
They are ready to renounce you and the world
in order to live the blessed life of immortality.
Give honor, therefore,
to the Holy Spirit who is about to come upon them.
May He descend from heaven,
cleanse and hallow them in the sacred font,
and make their hearts the temple and dwelling-place of
      God.
So shall these servants of God,
freed from all stain of past sin,
give thanks to God without ceasing

and bless His holy name for ever,
through Christ our Lord.

All respond: AMEN.
The signing and laying on of hands are repeated for the third time, with the following words:

I exorcise you, unclean spirit,
in the name of the Father,
and of the Son,
and of the Holy Spirit,
and command you to come out of these servants of God.
Depart from them, cursed fiend!
He who commands you is the one who walked on the sea
and stretched out His hand to Peter
when he was about to sink.
He who commands you is the one
who opened the eyes of the man born blind,
and raised Lazarus to life
after he had been in the grave four days.
Remember then that you are damned,
and give honor to the living and true God,
to Jesus Christ His Son,
and to the Holy Spirit.

Finally one of the priests marks the candidates' foreheads with the sign of the cross, lays his hands on their heads and prays:

O Lord most holy,
Almighty Father and Eternal God,
the Author of light and truth,
I ask Your everlasting mercy
on behalf of these servants of Yours.

Enlighten them with knowledge of Yourself;
cleanse and sanctify them;
give them true wisdom;
make them worthy to receive the grace of baptism,
and help them to persevere
in firm hope,
an upright will,
and sound faith,
through Christ our Lord.

All respond: AMEN.

The Rendering of the Creed

After the exorcisms the candidates are instructed to put on their shoes and outer garments, and are then called by name to recite the Creed individually. Their sponsors accompany them to the bishop's chair, where they repeat the Creed to assure the bishop that they have memorized it and will be able to profess it without anxiety on Holy Saturday.

Chapter Ten

You must know what to believe before you can pray

What you have just recited, by the grace of God, is the orthodox statement of the Christian Faith, on which Holy Church is firmly established. You have received the Creed and rendered it back. Be sure that you keep it for ever in your minds and hearts. Say it over to yourselves when you get up in the morning, think of it as you walk down the street, remember it during meals. Let your heart meditate upon these precious words even while you are asleep.

Now according to the Church's tradition, after giving you the Creed we next go on to teach you the prayer our Savior gave us. This too must be learned by heart and recited next week; and this too must be repeated continually by all who embrace the Christian Faith.

There is a text of Scripture that says that all who call on the name of the Lord shall be saved (Joel 2:32). But, as Saint Paul says, how can people call on the name of the Lord unless they believe in Him? And how can they believe in Him if they have never heard of Him? (Rom. 10:13–15). This passage of Scripture explains why we do not teach you the Lord's Prayer until you have learned the Creed. We give you the Creed first so that you will know what to believe, and then the prayer so that you will know who it is you are praying to and what to ask Him for. Then you will be praying in faith, and your prayer will be heard.

The Lord's Prayer

The Gospel tells us how the disciples asked our Lord to teach them to pray, just as John the Baptist taught his disciples. In response to this request Jesus gave them a short formula which perfectly reflects the attitude Christians should have toward their heavenly Father. "This is how you should pray," He told them.

> OUR FATHER, WHO ART IN HEAVEN,
> HALLOWED BE THY NAME.
> THY KINGDOM COME,
> THY WILL BE DONE ON EARTH AS IT IS IN HEAVEN.
> GIVE US THIS DAY OUR DAILY BREAD,
> AND FORGIVE US OUR DEBTS,
> AS WE HAVE FORGIVEN THOSE WHO WERE IN DEBT TO US.
> AND LEAD US NOT INTO TEMPTATION,
> BUT DELIVER US FROM EVIL.

How simple this prayer is, without a superfluous word! Jesus warned us not to imagine that the longer and more eloquent our prayer the more likely it would be to be answered. Some people, by their verbosity, give the impression of wanting to make sure God knows all the facts and arguments of the case. But our Lord told His disciples: "Your Father knows all your needs before you ask Him" (Matt. 6:8). Don't be long-winded with the Lord; He knows all about it beforehand.

Why pray at all then, we might ask? If God knows what we need, will He not give us the things He knows to be necessary without our troubling to ask?

Yes, God does know the things we need, and He does want to give them to us. But He wishes us to pray for them because He wants us to appreciate His gifts and earnestly desire them; otherwise we should be like spoiled children who do not know how to value the good things they take for granted. Our desire for God's gifts is itself His gift; in fact the prayer Jesus taught us is simply the expression of the desire He has put into our hearts.

Every prayer you need to make is included in this short formula. Any request that cannot be reduced to one of the petitions of the Lord's Prayer ought not to be made at all.

Let us go through it now in detail.

OUR FATHER, WHO ART IN HEAVEN.

I say *Our Father;* soon you too will be saying *Our Father.* You will truly know God as your Father when you are born again. You have already been begotten by Him; in the baptismal font you will be born as His child.

Always remember that you have a Father in heaven. Adam, your natural father, passed on to you a life destined for the grave, but God, your heavenly Father, is offering you life without end. When you say *Our Father,* then, say it with all your heart. Since you have a Father in heaven, do not set your hearts on earthly things. You are about to become part of a great family, a family in which all are brothers and sisters: rich and poor, master and servant, mistress and maid, general and private soldier. Christians have earthly fathers in various walks of life, but all of them pray to their common Father in heaven.

If our Father is in heaven, our inheritance is there too. Moreover, we shall not have to wait for Him to die before we can receive it; we shall enjoy it with Him. We have to lose our earthly fathers before we can succeed to their estate, but we shall never be bereft of our heavenly Father. He is waiting for us to join

Him in heaven. Let us make sure we understand what to pray for, so as not to offend Him by asking for the wrong things.

Pray for God's glory

The first petition Jesus taught us to make to our heavenly Father is:

HALLOWED BE THY NAME.

But isn't this rather a strange thing to pray for? Why ask for God's name to be hallowed, when His name can never be anything but holy? Surely the name of God is eternally holy!

Yes, His name is holy in itself, but we pray that it may be hallowed *in us*—that is, that we may always hold God's name in reverence, never taking it in vain or treating it with contempt. We pray that our lives may glorify His name.

Your task on earth is to live the kind of life that will make others praise God's name when they see how His mercy and grace have been lavished upon you, how He has adopted you as His children and given you His Holy Spirit in order that you may grow to maturity. They will see too that if He chastises you it is for your correction, because He is rearing you as true sons and daughters who have the right to call God their Father.

In the same way, we know that if we lead a life unworthy of God's children, we cause His name to be blasphemed. Let that never happen to you. On the contrary, let your lives be such that the world may learn to praise the name of our God, who has raised you up to so great a dignity.

So then, when we pray *hallowed be Thy name* we are really praying for ourselves. We are asking that we ourselves should be holy, and so glorify our heavenly Father. At the moment of your baptism God's name will be hallowed in you. You will be cleansed, forgiven, born anew to a life of holiness and justice.

And after you have been baptized, the petition *hallowed be Thy name* will mean: May we never lose the precious gift you have given us!

The second petition of the Lord's Prayer is:

THY KINGDOM COME.

Why do we ask this? Surely God's Kingdom will come whether we pray for it or not? Scripture says God has an everlasting Kingdom; all creatures serve Him (Dan. 7:14). But in this prayer we are asking that God's Kingdom should come *in us* as well as in all the saints, that He may reign supreme in our hearts, and that we may be admitted to His heavenly Kingdom. Last week when we were thinking about the Second Coming of our Lord to judge the living and the dead, we learned that on the Last Day Jesus will say: "Come, blessed of My Father, inherit the Kingdom prepared for you from the beginning of the world." When we say *Thy Kingdom come* we are praying once again for ourselves, that we may have the right of entry into that Kingdom. God's Kingdom will inevitably come, but what good will it do us if we find ourselves excluded from it with the reprobate? So then, pray with all your hearts that you may live the kind of life that will qualify you for a share in the heavenly Kingdom promised to all God's saints.

The next petition is:

THY WILL BE DONE ON EARTH AS IT IS IN HEAVEN.

What does this mean? Will not God's will be done whether we pray for it or not? Have you not just been reciting in the Creed: *I believe in God the Father Almighty,* who can do all He pleases? If God is almighty, why pray that His will may be done?

What each of us is asking in this petition is this: May Your will be done in me and by me, let me never resist Your will, let there be no barrier between us. May I serve You on earth as the angels serve You in heaven, lovingly carrying out all Your wishes and never offending You. This is what we ask: that we may do God's will in love.

We can also think of this petition in terms of the heavenly Kingdom of the future, the Kingdom we hope to inherit on the Last Day. In that Kingdom there will be no opposition to God's will; sin will have been rooted out and the power of evil destroyed. We shall no longer be subject to assault and temptation, because we shall live the resurrection life. God's will and ours will be completely one. We shall think heavenly thoughts and desire the things that please God, because there will no longer be a single rebellious impulse within us.

Now while we are in this present life, our prayer must be that just as the will of God is to reign supreme in the heavenly Kingdom of the future, so, as far as is possible in this world, His will should reign supreme in our hearts now and prevent our ever deliberately choosing what is opposed to it. Absolute freedom from rebellious feelings is impossible in this life where we are subject to continual change, but our will must steadfastly refuse to give way to them. God does not command that feelings and passions should never stir within us, but that we should not let them rule us. Whether events are painful or pleasant, glorious or humiliating, whether they lift us up or cast us down, we must constantly set our hearts on pleasing our heavenly Father. Neither the pleasures nor the trials of this world are important; God's will is the one thing that matters. We count ourselves happy when we obey it, even if it means bearing all the troubles of this world, just as we count ourselves infinitely wretched if we disobey it, even if this world lavishes all its favors upon us.

Chapter Eleven

Pray for your own needs

We saw last time that the first three petitions of the Lord's Prayer are all directed toward the glory of our heavenly Father. Today we will look at the remaining petitions, which are requests for what we need on our journey through this world. The first of these is:

GIVE US THIS DAY OUR DAILY BREAD.

Give us your everlasting blessings, Lord, but give us also the things we need in this temporal life. You have promised us the Kingdom of heaven; do not refuse us your help in our earthly necessities. When we ask for our daily bread we are not asking for food only, but for everything else we need to sustain us here on earth. Rich and poor alike, all of us are beggars in the sight of God; everything we have comes from Him. He makes no distinction between us; He makes His sun rise on everybody, good and bad, and sends His rain on the just and the unjust alike. Whether you praise Him or blaspheme Him, He feeds you, because He waits patiently for sinners to turn to Him in repentance and does not condemn them while there is still hope of their conversion.

We all receive our daily bread from God, whether we are Christians or not. Without it we could not live. But there is another kind of bread, the bread God's children ask of Him. Our Lord referred to it in the Gospel when He told the Samaritan woman, "It is not good to take the children's bread and throw it to the dogs" (Matt. 15:26).

This is the bread of God's word. Yes, the inspired Scriptures are also our daily bread during our life on this earth. Man does not live by bread alone, but by every word that comes from the mouth of God. Bread for our stomachs, food for our minds: we ask both of our heavenly Father.

Yet again there is another kind of daily bread we pray for, the food of our souls. It is the sacred bread you will receive from the altar after your baptism. It is good to pray for this bread, and to ask that we may never be deprived of it on account of our sins. The faithful will understand what I mean, and you too will understand once you are baptized.

When our earthly life is over, we shall no longer need to make this petition. We shall no longer have any use for bread, because we shall never be hungry again. We shall no longer need the sacrament of the altar, because we shall be wholly united with Christ. We shall no longer need to read the Scriptures, because we shall see the Word of God Himself through whom all things were made. That Word is the bread of angels; He is their light and their wisdom. Not by studying a book do the angels receive knowledge of Him, but by contemplating Him directly; and so shall we. Then, in company with the angels, we shall break out into praise without ceasing.

Forgive us our debts

Let us move on now to the next petition.

FORGIVE US OUR DEBTS

AS WE HAVE FORGIVEN THOSE WHO ARE IN DEBT TO US.

All of us need to say this. We are all in debt, because we are all sinners. The debts we ask our heavenly Father to forgive are our sins.

Even your teachers and your bishop need to say this prayer; we too have a debt to pay. We do not claim to be sinless; if we did, we should deceive ourselves as well as you. Yes, even though we have already been baptized, we still owe God satisfaction for our sins, not because any of the sins we committed before our baptism remain unforgiven, but because we are continually falling into new sins and need to be forgiven again every day.

When we come up out of the baptismal font we are free of all sin. If we died there and then, we should have no further debt to pay. But because we have to go on living in this world after our baptism, we cannot avoid committing some sins through human frailty. Our weakness often makes us fall against our will. These sins are not big enough to make shipwreck of our lives; still they do, so to speak, let in a certain amount of water that needs bailing out, otherwise by degrees we should sink. This bailing out is effected by prayer to God and by loving service of our neighbors.

A short time ago you declared your faith in the forgiveness of sins. Now there are two kinds of forgiveness: the first is given only once, in baptism; the second we obtain whenever we say the Lord's Prayer and make this petition, *forgive us our debts*. Prayer to God and charity to others will cleanse us of our daily sins, so long as these are not the grave and deliberate sins that deprive us of our daily bread and lead to death and damnation—murder, apostasy, adultery, perjury, witchcraft, and the like. If Christians commit sins of that sort, the Church is obliged to exclude them from the sacrament of the altar. They are then in very grave danger, until and unless that excommunication is lifted.

But apart from these deadly sins, there are many lesser faults into which we are continually falling: hasty actions, unguarded words, conceited thoughts, laziness, cowardice, selfishness, impatience. We know only too well how easy it is to give way to such things. Our daily sins may not be very great, but there are a great many of them. This is why we need to pray daily *forgive us our debts,* so that we can have these daily sins forgiven and washed away.

Forgive your enemies

But notice there is a condition. We can only be absolved of our debts if we absolve those who are in debt to us. God says to us, "Forgive others, and I will forgive you. If you do not forgive, you are the one who is holding your guilt against you, not I."

God has made a pact with us. Whenever we say *forgive us our debts,* we must add: *as we have forgiven those who were in debt to us.* If we omit the second clause or say it insincerely, it is no use saying the first.

My brothers and sisters, believe me when I assure you that this is the most important clause in the whole of the Lord's Prayer. You are about to be baptized. Forgive anyone who has ever injured you. If you have any resentment in your heart against anyone else, at this very moment forgive that person from the bottom of your heart. Then when you go down into the font, you can be absolutely certain that all your debt of guilt will be wiped out, both the state of alienation from God that you inherited from Adam, and all your own personal sins as well. You will come up from the water free of all debt.

But those people who were formerly in debt to you must be equally free. Make sure you do not start demanding vengeance from anyone who may have wronged you in the past. Let your forgiveness be total. Just as all your sins have been cast into the depths of the sea, so let the wrongs others have done you be consigned to oblivion.

If anyone sins against you after your baptism, forgive him at once. Forgive in your heart, where God sees. People sometimes forgive with their lips but not in their hearts. They say the words out of convention or human respect, but cherish resentment in their hearts because they have no respect for God.

I implore you not to be so unkind to your own soul. The cruelest enemy in the world cannot do you as much harm as you do yourself by refusing to forgive him. He can injure your property or your family or your bodily health, but he cannot do the harm to your soul that you yourself can do.

My friends, I urge you to reach out and lay hold of this perfect gift of love, the love of enemies. Do not say to yourselves, "It is impossible." I can tell you this: I personally know Christians who genuinely love their enemies, through the power the Lord has given them. That same power is offered to you. If you tell yourself it is impossible, then you will not be able to do it. The first step is to believe it is possible, and then to pray that God's will may be done in you.

What good will it do you to witness your enemy's downfall? Choose rather to seek his good; pray for his healing. Pray that he will renounce his malice, and then he will no longer be your enemy. After all, it is not his human nature that is hostile toward you. He has a soul and body like yours, he is made of the same clay as you yourself, and God has breathed the breath of life into him as he did to you. We are all descended from the same human stock; Adam is our father and Eve our mother. We belong to the same family. And now that we are Christians, God is our Father and the Church our mother; we are all brothers and sisters in Jesus Christ.

If you tell me your enemy is an unbeliever, I shall remind

you that you have just been praying *Thy will be done on earth as it is in heaven.* Pray to your Father in heaven for the conversion of your enemy who is still chained to the earth. Remember that Saul was the enemy of the first Christians, but when they prayed for him, he not only gave over persecuting the Church but became one of its greatest apostles. You too must pray in the same way for your enemy; pray that his malice may die, but that he may live. Then you will have lost an enemy and gained a brother.

If we do not forgive, we must not count on receiving forgiveness ourselves. Understand this clearly. Anger is a normal human passion and there is no need to be ashamed of angry feelings, so long as we keep them within bounds. You can be angry, the psalm says, but do not sin (Ps. 4:5); that is, do not hold on to the anger in your heart, for if you do it will turn into hatred, which is a deadly sin. Anger is a mere shoot, while hatred is a great tree. Nevertheless, a shoot can grow into a tree if it is not rooted out straight away. By harboring evil suspicions and rash judgments we water that shoot, that first movement of anger and resentment, until it grows into a fully developed tree.

So although angry feelings are natural and not in themselves sinful, they must be dealt with immediately and not allowed to grow into the desire for revenge. Who are we to seek to be avenged? If God chose to be avenged on us, what would become of us? When your enemy comes to you and asks your pardon, forgive him at once. Is this so very difficult? I know it is hard to love someone when he is actually attacking you, but is it so hard to love him when he asks for forgiveness? Yet my ambition for you is even greater than this, for I would hope that even when you are suffering wrong you would turn to the Lord Jesus, recalling His own prayer for His enemies: "Father, forgive them; they do not know what they are doing" (Luke 23:34).

Perhaps you may protest that after all Jesus was the Lord, the Son of God, the Word Incarnate—what can be expected of a mere human being? Very well, think of your fellow-servant Stephen, who was stoned to death by his enemies. When they forced him to the ground he prayed: "Lord, do not hold this sin against them" (Acts 7:59).

Notice that Stephen's enemies were not asking his forgiveness. They were hurling stones at him. Yet he prayed for them. This is the kind of Christian I want you to be. Make this your aim; grow and mature in your new life and reach out for this perfect gift which is the love of one's enemies. Why go on dragging your heart in the dust? Lift it up to the Lord; believe in the power He has given you to overcome yourself. Love those who hate you, then all the world will know that you are the children of your Father in heaven.

Do not despair if you do not succeed at once. If you cannot yet love your enemy at the moment when he attacks you, at least love him when he repents. Welcome the person who comes to you and says: "I am sorry. I did wrong. Forgive me." If at that moment you refuse to forgive, you will have to omit the part of the Lord's Prayer that says *Forgive us as we forgive.* How can you make such a prayer? However, if you omit it you will not be forgiven yourself. And if you say it hypocritically you will not be forgiven either. The only way to find forgiveness for yourself is to pray the prayer and fulfill the condition.

If you do not forgive the person who asks pardon, you will be the loser, because he has a court of appeal he can turn to. He can go to your common Master and say: "Lord, I asked my fellow servant to forgive me and he refused. Please forgive me Yourself." So he will receive forgiveness and go out from his Master's presence absolved from debt, while you remain bound. When the time comes for the Lord's Prayer to be said and you reach the petition *Forgive us our debts, as we have forgiven those who were in debt to us,* the Lord will answer you: "You wicked servant! I forgave you all your debt when you pleaded with Me;

should you not have had pity on your fellow servant?" (Matt. 18:32, 33). My brothers and sisters, these words are in the Gospel; they are not the fruit of my imagination.

What if your enemy will not apologize?

Be ready to forgive him when he does, and pray that he may have a change of heart, so that he may be restored to you as your brother and friend.

Chapter Twelve

Trials and temptations

We must now turn to the last two petitions of the Lord's Prayer, even though there is a good deal more I could say on the subject of forgiveness.

The sixth petition is:

AND LEAD US NOT INTO TEMPTATION.

What exactly does this mean?

Scripture has a lot to teach us about temptation. There is a passage in the letter of Saint James that begins: "When anyone is tempted, let him not accuse God of tempting him" (James 1:13). Saint James is speaking here about those temptations the devil uses to ensnare us so that he can get us into his power again. However, there is another kind of temptation which is strictly speaking not a temptation but a test—indeed this petition can be translated: "And do not put us to the test."

During our earthly life we are constantly encountering trials: sickness, financial difficulties, all kinds of annoyances and worries. We can become so burdened and harassed by them that we are almost ready to give up the struggle. *Lead us not into temptation* is a plea for preservation from all these trials, or at least for the courage to endure them bravely without giving way to impatience or despair. Of this kind of temptation Scripture says, "The Lord your God is testing you, to find out whether you really love Him" (Deut. 13:3).

Trials and temptations are sent to train us to be courageous Christians and athletes for the Lord. We should not ask our heavenly Father to spare us ordinary difficulties, but only to keep us safe from temptations that are beyond our strength, and not to abandon us to the power of the evil one.

God is never the source of temptations to sin. However, as Saint Paul says to the Romans, God does give some people up to their own desires as a judgment upon them (Rom. 1:24). When He does that, the Tempter triumphs; finding no opposition, he easily persuades such persons to give way to their own sinful inclinations. For Saint James goes on to teach us that temptation arises from our own selfish lust, which lures us away from the love of God into the path leading to self-gratification. Lust then conceives, says Saint James, and gives birth to sin (James 1:14, 15). The lesson is clear: we have to resist our own desires when they tempt us to turn aside from obedience to the Lord.

You may be surprised to learn that even after you are born again selfish desires can still be present in you. Now you must realize that these desires in themselves are not sinful; they are simply human. However, they have a tendency to gain control over us if we do not discipline them. This tendency remains in us after our sins have been wiped out in baptism. It is by resisting our selfish desires that we grow strong in the Lord's service. The way to deal with them is to make sure you are led by the Spirit, not by the impulses of your lower nature.

In your new life you will have nothing to fear from the devil; his power is broken, and he can do nothing against a baptized child of God. Your battle will be against your own lower nature.

Conquer yourself, and you have conquered the world. Neither the devil nor any of his agents can force you to sin against your will. Let us say someone offers you a bribe in the hope of corrupting you; if you have closed the door of your heart to avarice he will have no success. Only the person with an itching palm will be tempted by the bribe and fall into the trap.

Or let us say you meet an attractive person of the opposite sex who is already married; if you have brought your sexual desires under control, you will not fall into sin. Again, the devil may try to persuade you of your own virtue and importance, but if you shut the door to pride you will go your way unscathed. Yes, shut the door against every temptation, and bolt it with the love of God.

Who can do this without the help of our heavenly Father? That is why we pray *Lead us not into temptation.* After this we add the final petition,

BUT DELIVER US FROM EVIL

which is only another way of praying that we may not succumb to temptation and fall into sin. It is also a plea for protection against the manifold evils of this world in which we have to live.

If God is for us, who can be against us?

Have no fear. Your heavenly Father will hear your prayer and keep you safe. Not many days from now He will take away all your sins, giving you a full and perfect pardon for every wrong thing you have ever done. You can have absolute confidence in the Lord's power to defend you against your adversary the devil, and to protect you from all the snares by which he tries to make you sin against God.

Commit yourselves wholly to Jesus Christ; let Him be your Lord, then you need have no fear of the evil one. If God is for us,

Scripture says, who can be against us? (Rom. 8:31). All praise and glory to Him, now and for ever! The Lord will most certainly keep the promise He made us when He said that if we sought first the Kingdom of God and His righteousness, everything else we need would be given to us.

Just as you learned the Creed last week, I want you now to repeat the Lord's Prayer to yourselves during the coming days. Then when you join the faithful as they stand before God's altar saying the Lord's Prayer together, you will be able to pray it with them, in the joy of a newborn child of God.

Heavenly Father,
we have made known to these servants of Yours
the prayer Your Son gave us.
We know, Lord, that You are able
to bring them to new life in the waters of baptism.
We humbly ask that we ourselves
who have taught them the faith
may enter with them into Your heavenly Kingdom.
We ask this through Your only Son, Jesus Christ our Lord.
Amen.[10]

V
THE MEANING OF
BAPTISM

Chapter Thirteen

Jesus gives us right of entry into the heavenly Kingdom
Time is now getting short, and we must think about the
nature of the sacraments and the meaning of the rites connected
with them. These things must be explained if you are to know
the power of the Christian mysteries. If the grace they imparted
were self-evident, you would need no instruction; it would be
enough simply to tell you what will take place. But since sacraments are outward signs of inward realities, it is necessary to
learn the meaning of the signs and what they signify.

The Law contained only a shadow of the good things to
come; it did not express their full reality (Heb. 10:1). In the tent
erected by Moses the people served a copy and shadow of the
heavenly sanctuary, as we read in the Letter to the Hebrews
(Heb. 8:5). This tent consisted of an outer part known as the
Holy Place, which represents our present life on earth, and an
inner sanctuary called the Holy of Holies, which was a figure or
symbol of heaven, where our Lord Jesus Christ has gone before
us to sit at the right hand of the Father. The Jewish high priest
was only permitted to enter the Holy of Holies once a year.
He could not remain there because he was only a mortal man,
any more than we, as mere mortals, had access to heaven

before our Lord Jesus Christ made it possible for us.

But now Jesus has entered the true Holy of Holies by ascending to heaven. He entered first on our behalf as our eternal High Priest, and has opened the way for us to follow Him. He gives us right of entry by giving us a share in His own death and Resurrection. Jesus our brother submitted to the law of death for our sake, and triumphed over that law by rising from the dead. He can never die again, nor can He be touched by suffering or corruption, and He has promised that we too shall be as He is.

He has made His Church responsible for our admission

In the life of the resurrection we shall live in heaven, where Jesus has established His Kingdom. This Kingdom is the heavenly Jerusalem, the city of the living God; it is full of angels and the adopted children of the resurrection; Scripture calls it the Church of the Firstborn whose names are written in heaven (Heb. 12:23). However, this will only be fully perceived in the future when Jesus takes us up to heaven with Him and we are recognized as citizens of His Kingdom, enjoying full freedom of the city and exemption from suffering. There we shall enjoy all the good things of the Kingdom. Meanwhile, baptism gives us a foretaste on this earth of these heavenly realities.

In baptism we are symbolically buried with Christ and symbolically raised with Him to new life. As Saint Paul says, "We who have been baptized in Christ Jesus have been baptized into His death. We have been buried with Him in baptism in order that as Jesus has been raised from the dead to the glory of the Father, so we too may live a new life" (Rom. 6:3, 4). This text clearly shows that the meaning of our baptism is to make us one with Christ in His death and Resurrection.

In order to enter into this experience and obtain the right of entry into the Holy of Holies, we have to present ourselves to the Church of God, because Jesus bequeathed the power to dispense the sacraments to the Church He founded on the rock of Peter. He has made His Church responsible for admitting applicants to citizenship of the Kingdom of heaven. This is done by means of a symbolic rite, a sign which actually contains and confers the reality it signifies.

Accordingly it is necessary for you to present yourself to the Church in order to be enrolled as a citizen of the heavenly Jerusalem. This you have already done; the bishop who received your name made enquiries into your manner of life, to see if you were worthy and if you were prepared to renounce the evil practices of this world and live according to the laws of your new city. Since you were an outsider, one of the citizens took you to the bishop to testify to your worthiness and to act as your guide and instructor in the customs of the city.

Your sponsor does not make himself responsible for the sins you may commit in the future, for each of us will have to speak for himself before God; but he testifies to your present state and guarantees that you have prepared yourself as far as you can for membership in the city. The Church makes sure you understand clearly that, once baptized, you will not be free to abandon your citizenship. Since your name will be written in heaven, you will be expected to repudiate worldly ambitions and observe the laws of the heavenly city, paying your taxes to the king by living in accord with your baptismal grace.

Everyone must be enrolled

Let me give you an analogy to help you understand this better. When the Romans took possession of Judea, they ordered everyone in the country to be enrolled for purposes of taxation. Everyone hurried off to be registered in his own home town. Joseph and Mary went to Bethlehem to be registered, because they belonged to the family of David. In the same way everyone who believes in Jesus Christ must be enrolled in the registers of the Church, because Jesus, having conquered the devil and delivered the human race from his power, has established us under His own authority. All who acknowledge and submit to His rule ask to be baptized in order to have their names registered in heaven. So the bishop inscribes their names in the Church's register, together with the names of their sponsors.

However, they do not receive a certificate of membership until they have been examined and have shown themselves eligible for admission. They have to submit their petition to the divine administration in order to be released from their present ruler. Only then will they be free to enjoy the benefits of their new citizenship.

The enemy opposes our petition

To vary the analogy, imagine an earthly ruler who takes a census of all his subjects according to their provinces. One of them asks to be transferred to another district where the soil is very fertile and the residents enjoy many advantages. Now the petitioner has a long-standing enemy who hears of his request and is consumed with envy, since he once held that particular territory and occupied it for many years. So he appeals against the man's petition, claiming that he has the right of ownership and has been unjustly robbed and evicted. If the petitioner has really set his heart on the transfer, he must be prepared to take the matter to court and have it settled by law.

So it is with us. God has offered the Kingdom of heaven to the human race; He wants to give us eternal life and make us permanent citizens of His Kingdom. We can obtain these blessings in this world by means of sacramental signs which God has entrusted to His Church. Accordingly we must apply to the Church for enrollment as candidates for baptism. By this application we, so to speak, initiate legal proceedings against the tyrant who is fighting our claim—our old enemy Satan, who envies our happiness. He complains that we have no right to leave his jurisdiction; we have belonged to him by hereditary right ever since the fall of the first man and woman.

Our plea, however, is that the case has already been fully examined and the verdict pronounced in our favor. Satan has no further claim on us. Through Jesus Christ, we have in all justice been restored to our Lord's jurisdiction. It was to Him we belonged by right from the beginning and in His image we were originally created. We did indeed lose this dignity by our own folly, but God has now given it back to us. By His grace we no longer belong to this dying world; we have a lawful title to the citizenship of heaven. We have come to know the Lord. So we now eagerly apply for our certificate of membership of His Kingdom and the first installment of all His promised gifts. We present ourselves to the Church to be baptized, in order to be set free from the claims of the evil one and to receive the gift of eternal life.

Chapter Fourteen

The Church pleads our cause

Last time we spoke about our application for membership in the heavenly city, and how Satan opposes our claim. We saw that the verdict has already been given in our favor, and that all we need do now is present ourselves for baptism.

Of course you know that when anyone appeals to a judge for freedom from a cruel and unjust oppressor, he does not plead his own cause. It is another man's office to act as advocate and prove the plaintiff's rights by invoking the law of the land. He will use all his skill to procure a favorable verdict. The plaintiff must remain silent in an attitude of humble supplication while the whole matter is investigated and the facts are established. The proceedings are often lengthy, but the plaintiff must endure it all patiently.

When you gave in your name for baptism at the beginning of Lent, you made it quite clear that you wished to be set free from the devil's tyranny. But as you were incapable of extricating yourself from his bondage unaided, you had recourse to the ministry of the Church. Through her exorcists and priests, the Church has been pleading your cause for many weeks now. During all that time you were instructed to occupy your mind with the articles of the Creed and to learn them by heart. Adam and Eve were easily overcome by the serpent because they did not bear God's commandment in mind; therefore you were told to make sure the Creed was really fixed in your memory. Unless you thoroughly know and love your holy faith, you cannot receive or hold onto the gift of God.

The end of the trial is now in sight. The Judge has heard the evidence and listened to the arguments of both parties. Very soon now He will pronounce His decision in your favor and condemn the usurper. Before He does so, however, you will be asked to confirm your request by making a public renunciation of Satan and a commitment of your life to Jesus Christ in the presence of the bishop, whom the divine Judge has appointed to represent Him.

The Renunciation of Satan

According to ancient tradition, you begin by removing your outer garments and standing barefoot on sackcloth with hands outstretched. This posture signifies your former captivity and your desire to be rescued from it. As you stand there, you are instructed to pronounce the words:

> I RENOUNCE SATAN
> AND ALL HIS ANGELS,
> ALL HIS SERVICE,
> ALL HIS VAIN POMPS, AND ALL HIS WORLDLY ALLUREMENTS.
> I COMMIT MYSELF TO JESUS CHRIST
> AND PLEDGE MY ALLEGIANCE TO HIM.
> I BELIEVE,
> AND I ASK TO BE BAPTIZED
> IN THE NAME OF THE FATHER
> AND OF THE SON
> AND OF THE HOLY SPIRIT.

I want to explain in advance the efficacy of these words, so that you will fully understand the terms of the contract by which you are to obtain the privilege of your new citizenship.

Since obedience to the devil has caused untold evil to the human race, and you have experienced his malice in your own life, you must promise to turn away from him absolutely. Accordingly you say:

I RENOUNCE SATAN.

Up till now you would not have dared to say such a thing even if you had wanted to, for fear of what Satan might do to you. But thanks to the exorcisms, the divine Judge has decreed that you should be set free, and this has given you confidence to renounce the devil with your own lips. By saying *I renounce Satan* you are making two things clear: first, that you have up till now been associated with him, and second, that you now turn your back on him. No one can renounce a thing he has never had any part in. It is necessary to insist on this renunciation, because your membership in the human race has involved you in a hereditary fellowship with Satan; up till now you have been part of a wicked confederacy with him and have been subject to his cruel domination.

Now that you have received the power to escape from his service, you declare that you renounce him, meaning: "I will have no further association with him. I realize the evil things he has forced me to do in the past; I realize how he injured Adam and Eve, the parents of us all, who believed his lies; I realize to what a state of wickedness Satan has sunk, together with all those who have gone over to him, and what torments those people endure who choose to become his slaves. But I also realize the great and wonderful grace Jesus Christ is offering me: the grace of deliverance from the usurper's tyranny and of blessings beyond all imagining. I understand now where the source of all blessing is; I know my Lord and Savior. He is truly the Lord of my life; He made me out of nothing and has never ceased to show kindness to me. Even when I rebelled against Him He never abandoned me. He has offered me a marvelous gift: not only the end of my misery but also the hope of unimaginable happiness. From now on I will have nothing to do with Satan. I renounce him and shun him as a hateful malefactor who has caused all of us untold harm. He does not even know how to do good, but uses all his talents to hurt us and reduce us to slavery. But I no longer fear his power, because the Lord Jesus has destroyed it by becoming my brother and sharing my flesh and blood. He has conquered death by dying Himself, and so saved me from everlasting bondage."

This is the meaning of *I renounce Satan.*

Renunciation of Satan's agents

Now if Satan alone were our adversary, this renunciation would suffice. But though he himself is invisible, he can use visible means to injure us. At the beginning of the world the devil had no fallen men or women whom he could employ, so he used a serpent to seduce our first parents. Then when he had ensnared human beings, he used them to harm others.

People who try to turn Christians away from the Lord are fulfilling the same function that the serpent fulfilled in the Garden of Eden. So after you have renounced Satan you must add:

AND ALL HIS ANGELS

that is, all those men and women who have become tools of his malice for the downfall of others.[11]

We must count as angels of Satan those who try to make you revert to paganism, those who propagate atheism or false teaching, those who spread evil literature, those who try to persuade you either that Jesus is not truly God or that He did not truly become man, those who try to take away your faith or your trust or tell you your sins are unforgivable, or try to get you to do wrong and disobey God's will.[12] All these you renounce when you profess yourself a Christian. In future you must have no association with any of them. You have committed your life to Christ; you have been enrolled in the Church's register and are about to become a full member of the Body of Christ by being baptized. From now on you belong to Jesus Christ our Lord; He is your head.

Renunciation of superstition

After renouncing Satan and all his angels, you next add:

AND ALL HIS SERVICE.

Just as you have turned your back on all those who serve the evil one, so you must turn your back in horror on every kind of occult practice and dabbling in spiritualism. All such things are the service of Satan. Everything connected with pagan worship is a service of Satan; so is the practice of astrology, studying the position of the sun, moon, and stars before embarking on any journey or undertaking, imagining that their movements can bring good or bad luck, or resorting to fortune tellers. From all such things a Christian must turn away, fixing his eyes on God alone and depending on His providence. It is from God that a Christian expects all good things to come, and to God that he looks for the destruction of evil. He has no hope in anything apart from Him. He knows that putting his trust in superstitious practices is service of Satan, and will subject him to the devil's tyranny all over again. In fact, if, after renouncing Satan and making your contract with Christ, you involve yourself in these things once more, you will find Satan an even harsher master than before, because he will be smarting from the insults you have given him.

Next you say:

ALL HIS VAIN POMPS AND ALL HIS WORLDLY ALLUREMENTS.

Satan's vain pomps are every kind of performance designed to arouse people's baser passions and urge them to acts of cruelty or obscenity. The devil sows such things in the world under the guise of entertainment to lead men and women to ruin. It is easy to see the dangers of such pursuits. You must avoid such things now that you have obtained a share in the New Covenant and have been enrolled as citizens of heaven. You are coheirs with us of the good things to come, and must live in a way that is worthy of your inheritance.

Commitment to Jesus Christ

So then, you renounce Satan and all his angels, all his service, his vain pomps and worldly allurements. You reject him altogether and make it quite clear that you will never again have anything to do with him. Then you firmly declare:

I COMMIT MYSELF TO JESUS CHRIST
AND PLEDGE MY ALLEGIANCE TO HIM.

By this declaration you proclaim that in future you intend to remain close to the Lord, that you will be unshakable in your resolution never to abandon Him on any account, and that for the rest of your life the privilege of belonging to Him and walking with Him will be more precious to you than anything else in the world.

After this you must add:

I BELIEVE

because Scripture tells us that anyone who wants to draw near to God must first of all believe that He exists (Heb. 11:6). God is invisible, and faith is demanded of anyone who commits his life to Him and promises to walk with Him. Invisible too are the blessings faith prepares you to receive in heaven, thanks to the saving work of our Lord Jesus Christ. You must be absolutely convinced that God will give you the pledge of these unseen gifts in baptism.

That is why, after saying *I believe,* you go on to say:

AND I ASK TO BE BAPTIZED

because it is with firm faith in what is in store for you that you come forward for baptism—faith that by symbolically dying with Christ and rising again with Him you will be born again to new life and obtain the right of entry to the Kingdom of heaven. The fact is that as long as you are still mortal it is impossible for you to enter the Kingdom. It is only when you throw off your mortality in the baptismal font that you truly become a citizen of heaven and coheir of the Kingdom.

To all this you add:

IN THE NAME OF THE FATHER AND OF THE SON
AND OF THE HOLY SPIRIT

because this is the name of the God who made us and renews us. He who existed from all eternity and is the Creator of all things is three Persons in one God, the most blessed Trinity. To this God in Trinity you commit your lives; in the name of the Trinity you pronounce your vows, promising fidelity for ever. As you go down into the water you invoke the Trinity, and from the Trinity you trust that you will receive in heaven the good things you now receive in symbol and anticipation on earth, and that you will enjoy them for ever after the resurrection of the dead, when you will be immortal by nature and share in the inheritance of your heavenly home.

The spiritual sealing

When you have made your renunciation and commitment, each of you will be taken to the bishop, before whom you will recite the Creed. Then, as you kneel before him, the bishop will make the sign of the cross on your forehead with chrism, saying:

> I SIGN YOU IN THE NAME OF THE FATHER
> AND OF THE SON
> AND OF THE HOLY SPIRIT.

This is the first installment of the sacrament he is administering to you, and he begins by invoking the blessed Trinity, the source of all our blessing.

The reason for this first anointing is that the devil is furious at what is happening. He is pacing to and fro like a roaring lion, gnashing his teeth at the sight of his former slaves deserting him and enlisting in the army of Jesus Christ. So the bishop signs your forehead with the seal which marks you as a Christian. From this seal a spiritual light blazes out, so dazzling that the devil dare not look you in the face for fear of being blinded, and in consequence he is deterred from molesting you in future.

Or you can, if you prefer, think of the seal as resembling the mark with which a shepherd brands his sheep. Whatever image you employ, the meaning is the same; the person who is thus sealed is marked out as belonging to Jesus Christ. It signifies that you have been accepted by God, who has pronounced His verdict in your favor and given you freedom of access to Him and the privilege of entering His presence with unveiled face.

When the sealing is completed, you rise from your knees to show that you have left your fallen condition behind. God has granted your petition and accepted your homage. He has chosen you for spiritual service and has summoned you to heaven, where from now on you must dwell in spirit, detached from earthly things. You now carry your identification mark as a soldier of Jesus Christ; accordingly you may receive the remaining sacramental rites and so be fully equipped with the armor of the Spirit.

Chapter Fifteen

Water and the Spirit

When we left off last time, we had reached the point where you are marked with the spiritual seal that signifies your acceptance by God. Today we come to the actual baptism. I want to explain this in detail, because it is the most important moment of your whole life.

You must realize that we human beings are made of body and soul, and for that reason we need a twofold cleansing. Our bodies need washing with water, and our souls must be purified and sealed by the Holy Spirit. So when you see the water in the baptismal font, do not think of it as mere water; think of the saving power with which the Holy Spirit has endowed it.

There is no other way to become a Christian than by water and the Spirit. This is the way the Lord Jesus determined that we should be born again, and it is not for us to find fault with the means He chose. Both water and the Spirit are necessary. A person can be baptized with water, but if God sees that his heart is not right he will not receive the grace of the Spirit. On the other hand someone may be a very good person, but unless he is sealed by the Spirit in sacramental baptism, he cannot enter the Kingdom.

This seems very bold language, but I can only say it is the Lord's, not mine. In confirmation of it, think of the story of Cornelius in the Acts of the Apostles. Cornelius was a good man, and on familiar terms with the angels. His prayers and acts of kindness did not go unnoticed by God, who sent Peter along to explain the good news to him. As Peter was talking, the Holy Spirit fell on Cornelius and his friends just as He had fallen on the Apostles at Pentecost; they began praising God in tongues and prophesying. Yet notice that even though they had received the gift of the Holy Spirit, Peter gave orders that they were to be baptized with water, so that they would be incorporated into the Body of Christ which is His Church. Thus their bodies would share in the new life of the resurrection which faith had brought to their souls.

Everyone who desires to be saved must receive baptism. The only exception is for martyrs who are baptized in their own blood. Jesus taught us that martyrdom was equivalent to baptism when He asked James and John if they could drink His chalice and be baptized with His baptism. But everyone else must enter the Kingdom by being born again in the sacramental waters.[13]

At the general resurrection of the dead on the Last Day, this new birth will be visibly manifested. In the meantime, through faith in Jesus Christ, we receive new life by means of signs and symbols. However, these signs and symbols are not empty ceremonies; they are charged with reality. They give us here and now a real, valid share in what is to come. We receive new life in the spirit even while we are still in this world, and the resurrection of our bodies in the next. Baptism is the symbol of both.

Jesus Himself described it in these terms when He said to Nicodemus: "Unless a man is born anew, he cannot enter the kingdom of heaven" (John 3:5). Nicodemus took this to mean that he had somehow to return to his mother's womb and go through the natural birth process all over again. So Jesus clarified His meaning by explaining: "Unless a man is born of water and the Spirit, he cannot enter the kingdom of God."

Baptism is a symbolic birth that believers must undergo in order that, by means of the sign, they may possess the reality it signifies. Water is the sign; the Spirit is the agent. Jesus went on to say: "What is born of the flesh is flesh, and what is born of the Spirit is spirit" (John 3:6). In other words, by your birth in the flesh you are naturally subject to weakness, pain, and death, but when you are born of the Spirit you will become by nature free from all these afflictions.

Saint Paul says that all of us who have been baptized into Christ Jesus have been baptized into His death. In baptism we die and are buried with Him, so that as Christ has been raised from the dead in the glory of the Father, we too may begin to lead a new life (Rom. 6:3, 4). Before the Incarnation death ruled over us by divine decree, and we could not break its hold. But by His own death and Resurrection the Lord Jesus delivered us from death's stranglehold. When believers die now, it is as though they fall into a prolonged sleep. Saint Paul calls Christ "the first fruits of those who have fallen asleep" (1 Cor. 15:20). He means that those who die after Christ's Resurrection will rise again as Christ did, because Christ has abolished death. Because we believe this we come to Him to be baptized; we want to share His death so as to share His risen life. When I am baptized and plunge my head into the water, I do so in the intention of embracing Christ's death and burial, and I solemnly declare my faith in His Resurrection. Then when I come up out of the water I count myself to be already risen.

What a marvelous gift baptism is! Christ was actually crucified, His soul was separated from His body, He was truly buried and rose again, and by imitating these things symbolically we gain salvation in reality! Jesus suffered for us in reality, not just in appearance, while we only share in the likeness of His suffering and death. Yet our share in His risen life is given us in reality, not just in appearance. This is why Saint Paul does not say, "We have been planted together in His death," but "in the *likeness* of His death" (Rom. 6:5, emphasis added).

Your new birth is the work of the Holy Spirit of God, whom you receive in the sacrament as a pledge. You can understand now how important, how wonderful, and how awe-inspiring this sacrament is. As Saint Paul says, "We who believe in Christ have been sealed with the Holy Spirit of the promise as the guarantee of our inheritance in His glory" (Eph. 1:13, 14). He also says: "God has set His seal upon us and has given us His Spirit in our hearts as a guarantee" (2 Cor. 1:21, 22); and in the Letter to the Romans we read that "we who have the first fruits of the Spirit here on earth groan inwardly during the time of our waiting for God to make us fully His children by setting our bodies free" (Rom. 8:23). All these texts confirm that we have the first fruits of the Spirit here on earth; in heaven, when our bodies have risen from the dead and we have become immortal, immune to further suffering or corruption, we shall have the fullness.

The stripping and anointing

Yesterday I explained the initial sealing with holy oil which marks you out as a soldier of Jesus Christ. In the next step of the rite, you strip completely. This is a sign that you are now putting off your old nature with its sinful practices (Col. 3:9). You are also imitating Jesus as He hung naked on the Cross, where He disarmed the principalities and powers of darkness, publicly triumphing over them (Col. 2:15).

In addition to this symbolism, the clothing you take off also represents your mortality, since Adam and Eve were originally naked and unashamed, and only needed clothes after they had become mortal through disobedience. You present yourself for baptism in order to be born again to immortal life, and so you remove your clothes. When you have done this, you will be anointed with oil from head to foot, as athletes of Christ preparing to enter the spiritual arena, or as soldiers receiving spiritual armor against the enemy's weapons. This oil is called the "oil of exorcism," because through the invocation of God's name and the bishop's prayer it is invested with power to repel the attacks of evil spirits.

The descent into the font

After this a deacon takes you by the hand and leads you down into the sacred font. The font contains no common or ordinary water, but the waters of regeneration. Ordinary water has been changed by the coming of the Holy Spirit. The bishop came beforehand and, in the traditional words of the Church, prayed that the grace of the Holy Spirit might come upon the water and make it the womb of sacramental birth, capable of engendering new life. This is the meaning of our Lord's words to Nicodemus. Just as in natural birth the mother's womb receives the seed but it is God who fashions it, so in baptism the water is the womb that receives the person about to be reborn, but it is the Spirit that fashions him and makes him a new creation.

Consider the seed that enters the mother's womb. It has no life of its own, neither has it a human soul or the capacity to feel. But in the womb God forms it into a living person, so that when in due course it emerges, it is endowed with a nature capable of every human activity. The same thing happens in baptism. A person enters the font as if he were a seed entering a kind of womb. He is baptized and fashioned by the Holy Spirit into a new creature. His whole nature is changed. Once he was doomed to death and corruption; now he is wholly immune to them and to the changing conditions of this world. This marvelous transformation is accomplished in the water by the power of the Holy Spirit.

Now although a baby is born with the capacity to speak, walk, and use his hands, he cannot immediately exercise these faculties. First he must grow and gain strength, learning gradually to use his natural endowments, until the day comes when he has the full use of his human powers. In the same way a person is reborn in baptism with all the potentialities of an immortal nature, but is incapable of using them effectively until the time is ripe. Then, at God's decree, all of us will rise from the dead and enter into full possession of our immortality. We shall know perfect freedom from pain, inconstancy, and every kind of weakness. The power of the Holy Spirit will make our bodies imperishable and glorious and our souls strong and inviolable. As Saint Paul tells the Corinthians, bodies sown in weakness will be raised in power and splendor; sown as natural bodies, they will rise as spiritual bodies (see 1 Cor. 15:42).

Clearly it is not in the nature of water to work such a transformation. It is effected by the grace of the Holy Spirit. That is why the bishop prays that the Spirit will endow the water with power to bring men and women to new birth in a higher nature.

Why water?

The reason this whole process takes place in water is that man was originally molded out of clay, which is a mixture of earth and water. When he sinned his nature was flawed; he became like a spoiled vessel, useless for its maker's purpose.

In the Bible God tells the Prophet Jeremiah to go to the potter and watch him at work. Whenever the shape of one of the potter's vessels displeased him, he would flatten it out and reshape it, dipping it in water a second time. After Jeremiah had watched him at work for a while, God said to him: "Can I not do the same with you, house of Israel?" (Jer. 18:2–6).

We too are vessels of clay, spoiled by sin and displeasing to God. Death has brought decay and dissolution upon us, and, as it were, flattened us out; but our Creator has decreed that we should be dipped in water so that He can fashion us anew.

The clay Jeremiah watched the potter shaping was soft and plastic, capable of being remodeled as often as he chose. But when the potter was satisfied with it, he put it into the kiln for firing. There it was baked hard, unchangeably set in the form he had given it. It could then last indefinitely unless it was broken. In the same way, we who are mortal, fickle, and always tending toward dissolution are renewed and formed afresh in the waters of baptism. We receive the grace of the Holy Spirit, a fire which hardens us more than any potter's kiln, making us immortal, imperishable, and permanently sealed in our character as children of God.

We have likened the font to a womb, and again to a crucible. It is also like a grave in which you are buried with Christ in the earth and rise again with Him to new life. So rich is the symbolism of baptism that it can be expressed in all these ways. But the giver of these wonderful blessings—the one who forms you, shapes you, recasts you, raises you to new life—is always one and the same, the blessed Trinity, Father, Son, and Holy Spirit.

The triple immersion

So then, the deacon or deaconess takes you by the hand and leads you down into the water. One of the priests standing there lays his hand on your head and asks you:

DO YOU BELIEVE IN GOD THE FATHER ALMIGHTY?

You reply:

I DO BELIEVE.

Then he gently pushes you down into the water, immersing your head. When you lift your head again he asks you:

DO YOU BELIEVE IN JESUS CHRIST,
HIS ONLY SON, OUR LORD,
WHO DIED FOR YOU AND ROSE AGAIN?

You reply:

I DO BELIEVE,

and he immerses you a second time. Finally he asks:

DO YOU BELIEVE IN THE HOLY SPIRIT?

For the third time you reply:

I DO BELIEVE

and for the third time your head is plunged in the water. By these symbolic actions you are buried and reborn. The one who baptizes you addresses you by name, saying:

YOU ARE BAPTIZED
IN THE NAME OF THE FATHER AND OF THE SON
AND OF THE HOLY SPIRIT.

This formula corresponds to our Lord's instruction, "Go and teach all nations, baptizing them in the name of the Father, and of the Son, and of the Holy Spirit" (Matt. 28:19). We are simply the ministers of this great sacrament. Its effects are produced by the blessed Trinity, the cause of all things, who created you out of nothing and now renews you and gives you immortal life.

You go down into the font once, but you are immersed three times. This teaches you that there is only one baptism; the grace given by Father, Son, and Holy Spirit is one and the same, for the three Persons of the Trinity are one single God and they act as one. It is this one God who adopts us as His children; in Him we believe, and in His name we are baptized, becoming a single body in the power of the Holy Spirit. The Spirit's power makes us children of God and members of Christ our Lord. Christ is our Head because He shares our humanity; He was the first man to rise from the dead in order that the rest of us might share His risen life. As Saint Paul says, Christ is the head from whom the whole body with all its joints and ligaments is nourished and knit together, and grows according to God's design (Col. 2:19).

Chapter Sixteen

You are now a child of God

Last time we reached the moment when you go down, naked, into the water and are baptized in the name of the Most Holy Trinity. After that, you come up from the font, a baptized child of God. You have been baptized into the death of Jesus.

As I have already told you, baptism is a real death, but not in a bodily sense. Jesus hung on the Cross for you in all its agonizing reality. He endured nails in His innocent hands and feet, suffering terrible pains; but He allows you to share in His death without agony or effort. He was physically buried in the earth; you are symbolically buried in the water. He rose again bodily to new life; you rise again symbolically when you come up from the font, born again, a completely changed person. From now on you no longer belong to Adam and the old way of life; you belong to Christ, who lives for God in perfect freedom from sin.

Now let us look at the remaining rites, which complete your initiation.

The white garment and chrismation

As soon as you come up from the water you are given a pure white garment. It is a sign of the new life you are to live as children of the resurrection, and of the purity and honesty that should now distinguish you. Then you come immediately to the bishop to receive that final sealing which completes and perfects your initiation and empowers you with the gifts of the Holy Spirit. In this you follow the example of Jesus Himself, who was baptized in the Jordan in order to make baptism a source of holiness for us. When He came up from the water the Holy Spirit came down and rested on Him in the form of a dove. This is why Jesus applied to Himself the prophecy of Isaiah, "The Spirit of the Lord is upon Me, and therefore the Lord has anointed Me" (Is. 61:1). Saint Peter too describes Him as "Jesus of Nazareth, whom God anointed with the Holy Spirit and with power" (Acts 10:38).

Jesus was the Son of God, yet He did not begin to preach the good news until He had been baptized. But from the moment when the Holy Spirit came down on Him in the shape of a dove, He began to proclaim the Kingdom of God and to do mighty works. If you commit your life to Jesus, the Holy Spirit will come down on you too, and the Father will say: "This is My adopted son." You will be a witness to Jesus, because you will be given the power to resist the forces of evil, just as Jesus overcame the temptations of Satan in the desert for forty days after His baptism. Before baptism you lack the strength to fight the devil, but once you have been born again you receive the power to fight with the weapons of righteousness in Jesus' name, and to spread the good news of salvation. You will put on the whole armor of God and be able to stand against all the power of the enemy and overcome it, saying, "I can do all things in Him who strengthens me" (Phil. 4:13).

So then, you come to the bishop to be chrismated. As he anoints you with chrism and lays his hand on your head, he says to you:

GOD THE FATHER ALMIGHTY HAS GIVEN YOU NEW BIRTH
BY WATER AND THE HOLY SPIRIT
AND HAS FORGIVEN ALL YOUR SINS:
HE HIMSELF NOW ANOINTS YOU FOR ETERNAL LIFE.

This sign shows that you are fully initiated and have the right to be called a Christian. God Himself has anointed you, marking you with His seal and giving you the pledge of His Spirit to carry in your heart (2 Cor. 1:21, 22). The Spirit is yours; He makes His home in you. In this present life you enjoy His indwelling as the first installment of the blessings which you will receive in all their fullness in the life to come.

What an anointing! Never let life in this world seem more important to you than the eternal life for which you have been anointed. No matter who attacks your faith or even threatens to kill you unless you agree to commit sin, never let your judgment become clouded. Choose the life for which you have been anointed, not the other. Choose eternal life, rather than the short life of this passing world.

Baptism is a guarantee of your resurrection

In that eternal life, as I have told you many times, there will be no more pain, no more dying, no more sorrow, no more temptation or sin. Baptism guarantees that we already have this resurrection life in sacramental signs, and so are assured of possessing it openly and tangibly in the future.

When you have received this new life in baptism, you must nourish it with the food of immortality at the holy altar of God. But of this we shall speak later. After the great night of Easter when all these things will happen to you, I want you to come here again every day for a whole week, wearing your new white garments, to receive further instruction in these wonderful mysteries, to learn how they were all foretold in the Scriptures, and to complete whatever remains to be explained about the new life in the Spirit in which you are to walk. But I have told you this much in advance, so that even before you experience these things you may know great happiness. Hope will give you wings and set your hearts on things above. Your thoughts will be transported from earth to heaven, from visible to invisible things, and with the eyes of the spirit you will see the reality of grace more clearly than the things that are apparent to your senses.

Rejoice in the Lord, my brothers and sisters, for your redemption is at hand! All the citizens of heaven are watching for your salvation to be accomplished. The Prophet Isaiah is calling to you: "Ho, all you who are thirsty, come to the waters!" (Is. 55:1). It will not be long before you are listening to that lovely passage, "Arise, Jerusalem, and be enlightened, for your light has come" (Is. 60:1). Your birthday is close at hand. Let all these teachings nourish and strengthen you, so that Mother Church may have the joy of bringing you forth to new life. Take all we have said to heart, beloved, and prepare in joy and humble trust to welcome the fullness of the baptismal gift.

During the next three days we shall all be fully absorbed in the commemoration of the Lord's Passion, death, and burial, and there will be no opportunity for further instruction. Wash yourselves in readiness for your new birth; observe the fast together with the whole Church of God; ponder in your hearts all that the Lord has suffered for you and the great love He shows you in calling you to new life in Him.

On Saturday afternoon you must all assemble in the vestibule for the rite of the Opening of the Ears. By the grace of this sign your spiritual ears will become receptive to the word of God; you will understand the mysteries about to take place, and become sensitive to the fragrance of the Spirit. After this, all we have told you about will take place in the customary order. Have no fear; the deacons will shepherd you, and your sponsors will support you and remind you of what you have to do.

I leave you now in silence and peace, securely wrapped in the remembrance of all these instructions, until the moment comes for your new birth.

Let us pray for our catechumens,
and ask our Lord and God to open the ears of their hearts
together with the gate of His mercy,
so that, born anew in the waters of baptism,
they may receive forgiveness of all their sins
and be incorporated into the Body of our Lord Jesus
    Christ.

Almighty and eternal God,
it is You who make Your Church continually fruitful with
    new offspring.
Increase the faith and understanding of our catechumens,
so that they may be born again in the baptismal font
and be numbered among Your adopted sons and
    daughters.
We make our prayer through our Lord Jesus Christ, Your
    Son,
who lives and reigns with You in the unity of the Holy
    Spirit,
one God, for ever and ever.
Amen.[14]

VI
THE RITES OF
INITIATION

The Rites of Initiation

On the Thursday of Holy Week the Oil of Exorcism and the Oil of Thanksgiving, or Chrism, are blessed by the bishop, and during Holy Saturday morning he blesses the baptismal water.

On Holy Saturday afternoon the candidates assemble in the vestibule for the Opening of the Ears. The bishop touches the ears and nostrils of each one, saying:

EPHPHATA: BE OPENED.

Then they enter the church, where they are instructed to remove their shoes and outer garments and to stand on sackcloth. The bishop now addresses them as follows:[15]

At last, my brothers and sisters, the end of your long preparation is in sight, and the time is at hand for your deliverance. This very day you are to produce the chart of your faith in the presence of our Lord Jesus Christ, a chart written on your own conscience and signed by your own tongue.

When people are about to die they draw up their last will and testament and nominate their heir. Now you are to die tonight, to die to sin. Accordingly you must take stock of your possessions and draw up your will. That is what this act of re-nunciation means. You are nominating the devil as heir to your sins and bequeathing them all to him as his inheritance.

So then, examine your hearts; if any of you finds anything belonging to the devil there, let him throw it out now before it is too late, because when a man dies he no longer has the power to dispose of his possessions. None of you must retain any of the devil's property in his heart. This is why you have been told to stand with your hands raised, so that the angels can search you to see if you still have any of Satan's goods on your person; to see if anyone has hatred or unforgiveness in his heart, or if any of you has come forward for baptism in a hypocritical spirit.

This is your last chance. Throw out everything unclean, every sinful habit. Pitch them all on to the devil. Look into your consciences, search your hearts. Let each one of you consider his past life, and if he still finds any of the devil's poison in him, let him spit it out. Let there be no pretense, no lack of faith in the power of this sacrament. The word of God searches your hearts more keenly than a two-edged sword.

Think of yourselves as slaves whom Jesus Christ is about to redeem. The devil is standing over there toward the west, the region of darkness, grinding his teeth, shaking his fist, and roar-ing with rage at finding himself deserted. He refuses to accept the fact that you have been saved. So you must stand facing him, look him in the eye, defy him, and blow a blast of breath in his face, as the first round of your struggle against him. Then you must turn to face the east, the source of light, and pledge your allegiance to Jesus Christ, the true light of the world.

Stand, then, in great reverence. This is the most solemn moment of your whole life. All the powers of heaven are present here. Angels and archangels are writing down everything you say. They are ready to receive your chart and carry it to the Master in heaven. Pay attention to every detail, so that you make no mistake. You are about to renounce your enemy, freely and deliberately, once and for all, and to commit yourself to your Creator.

Turn now toward the west. Lift up your hands, and repeat what I say:

> I RENOUNCE SATAN;
> I RENOUNCE ALL HIS ANGELS;
> I RENOUNCE HIS SERVICE;
> I RENOUNCE HIS VAIN POMPS
> AND ALL HIS WORLDLY ALLUREMENTS.

Repeat it three times after me. Now, answer me:
Have you renounced Satan?

> *All respond:* WE HAVE RENOUNCED HIM.

Very well; now blow upon him.[16]
Now turn to face the east. Lower your hands. Stand in great reverence and repeat what I say:

> I COMMIT MYSELF TO JESUS CHRIST
> AND PLEDGE MY ALLEGIANCE TO HIM.
> I BELIEVE,
> AND I ASK TO BE BAPTIZED
> IN THE NAME OF THE FATHER
> AND OF THE SON
> AND OF THE HOLY SPIRIT.

Repeat this three times after me. Now, tell me:
Have you committed yourselves to Jesus Christ?

> *All respond:* WE HAVE.

Thanks be to God! Now bow down and worship Him.

Blessed be the God whose will it is that all should be saved and come to the knowledge of the truth! All praise and glory to Him, now and for ever.

All respond: AMEN.

The candidates are next called individually to come forward and recite the Creed. As each person is summoned by the deacon, he is accompanied by his sponsor, who stands near him while he mounts the steps of a raised platform and, in the hearing of all the faithful, pronounces the text of the Creed word for word. This is his solemn rendering of the Creed and his profession of faith, which he will repeat in an abridged form as he stands in the baptismal font in a few hours' time.

The bishop now continues his address to the candidates.

Now, your chart has been signed. The Master has it in His safekeeping. Strive to keep all its clauses, because this chart of yours will be presented to you on the Day of Judgment. See that you do not have to blush before the dread tribunal on that day when the universe will be shaken and the entire human race will stand before its Judge. Millions of angels will be there, the whole army of heavenly spirits. You will see the burning lake of fire, the worm that never dies, the outer darkness; and this chart of yours will be read aloud.

If you have been generous and merciful, you will have advocates for your defense in those to whom you have shown kindness. But if you have been inhuman, grasping, ruthless, haughty, or unjust toward those who have done you no wrong, then the devil will rise up to accuse you. "Lord," he will say, "this person renounced me in words only. In his actions he has always been my servant." And then all the saints will burst into tears and all the angels will mourn over you. The final sentence is painful even to speak of.

Here on earth, if someone is in distress he can find advocates, he can call on his friends, his relatives will help him, his money will ransom him. But there nothing of the kind is possible. There will be no father to assist you, no mother to have pity on you, no brother or sister to come to your aid, no friends to support you. Each person will be naked, alone and without resources, with nothing but his own actions to succor or condemn him, because, as Scripture says, no one can pay his own ransom or pay God a price for his life (Ps. 49:8).

So keep watch over yourselves. You have renounced Satan; you must continue to shun him and everything connected with him right to the end. You have committed your lives to Jesus Christ; you must continue to testify to Him till your last breath. Die in the profession you have just made, and never make shipwreck of your faith. Have compassion on the poor, do not turn away from the victims of injustice, do not take what belongs by right to another, do no harm to little ones, do not listen to idle talk, support your pastors, and keep guard over your life in all circumstances.

My brothers and sisters, I have not hesitated to pronounce these sobering threats, because it is my duty to make sure you know what to guard against. I have done what I could. I have told you about these penalties beforehand, for fear that the enemy may suddenly attack and carry one of you off. You must realize that from now on he will take note of your words, your movements, and everything you do. So be on your guard, and then the enemy will have nothing to say against you on Judgment Day; and we, your ministers, will also be able to stand before the Lord's tribunal without shame and hear that glorious invitation: "Come, blessed of My Father, take possession of the Kingdom prepared for you from the beginning of the world."

After this the deacons instruct the candidates to put on their shoes and outer clothing. The bishop then prays for them:

Lord of all power,
set Your seal on the act
by which Your servants have committed themselves to
    You.
Keep them faithful to You throughout their lives.
Let them never be shaken in their allegiance.
Let them no longer be enslaved to evil
but serve the God of truth.
May they be Your subjects for ever;
may all who meet them recognize
that they belong,
body and soul, to You,
O Lord, Creator of all things.
This we ask through Your only Son, Jesus Christ.
Through Him may all glory and power be Yours
in the Holy Spirit,
now and for ever.
Amen.[17]

Next all who are to be baptized are summoned to come forward for the sealing. The bishop makes the sign of the cross with chrism on the forehead of each one, then he returns to the altar and prays:

God our Savior,
we know that You desire all mankind to be saved
and to come to the knowledge of the truth.
You, Lord, are the Truth;
may the knowledge of Your holy name
shine in our hearts
and in the hearts of these servants of Yours

who are preparing for baptism.
Give them Your imperishable gift
and unite them to the Holy, Catholic, and Apostolic
    Church;
for it is natural for You to be merciful and to save us,
since You are our God.
We praise You, Father, Son, and Holy Spirit,
now and for ever.
Amen.[18]

The candidates are then blessed and dismissed until the evening, when, together with all the people, they assemble in church for the sacred paschal vigil, called "the mother of all holy vigils." There they will spend the entire night watching and praying, as they wait in expectant faith for the Lord's Resurrection. The hours are filled with scripture readings, canticles, and prayers, while from time to time the bishop gives brief sermons and exhortations to encourage the people to stay awake.

Toward midnight the candidates make their way in procession toward the baptistery, singing the forty-second psalm:

As the deer longs for running streams,
so my soul longs for You, my God.
My whole being thirsts for God, the living God.
When shall I come into His presence
and see His face?

The font, already blessed by the bishop, is an octagonal-shaped pool let into the paved floor of the baptistery. It is adorned with symbolic representations of Paradise, where the Good Shepherd is portrayed leading His flock to heavenly pastures, and is sur-rounded by a gallery in which are curtained niches where the candidates take off all their clothes. They are then anointed from head to foot by deacons or deaconesses, and a priest says the follow-ing prayer:

Almighty Lord God of truth,
we know that You are merciful and compassionate
and that You love the work of Your hands.
We pursue You with our prayers,
because we put our trust in the promises
of Your only Son, who said:
"When You forgive men's sins,
they are forgiven";
We now anoint these servants of Yours
who have come to be born anew
in this holy sacrament.
We pray that our Lord Jesus Christ
may heal and strengthen them.
May He reveal His power to them,
through this anointing,
removing from them every trace of sin and wickedness
and all the effects of Satan's malice,
so that they may be cleansed and set free
in body, soul, and spirit.
May He pour out His grace and forgiveness upon them,
so that they may be dead to sin
and live in holiness.
May they be fashioned anew through this anointing,
molded afresh,
washed clean in this saving water,
renewed by Your Holy Spirit,
so that from now on
they may be impervious to the attacks of the enemy
and the allurements of this world.
So may they be gathered together

into the flock of our Lord and Savior, Jesus Christ,
and, with all Your holy ones,
share in the promised inheritance.
In His name we worship You, God our Father,
in the Holy Spirit,
now and for ever,
Amen.[19]

One by one the candidates are led down into the water and baptized. On emerging from the font, they put on white garments and sandals and present themselves to the bishop, who chrismates them.

When all have been baptized and chrismated, they return to the church in procession, carrying lighted candles and singing the forty-third psalm:

I will go to the altar of God,
the God who renews my youth and joy.

There they take their place next to the altar for the eucharistic liturgy. For the first time they are present for the whole of the eucharistic liturgy; they receive Holy Communion, the sacrament of the faithful, even though they have as yet had no instruction concerning the Eucharist. After communion they are also offered a chalice containing a mixture of milk and honey; according to ancient tradition this symbolizes the Promised Land, the food of newborn babes, and the sweetness of God's word.

They are now fully initiated Christians, welcomed with love and joy by all the faithful, and given a place of honor near the altar throughout the whole of Easter week. They are called "neophytes" (literally: newly planted), because although physically the same people, they are spiritually a new creation. For a whole week they wear their white garments and the entire community celebrates their new birth, surrounding them with special attention. In addition to the Easter sermons addressed to all the people, the neophytes hear daily lectures completing the prebaptismal teaching, explaining the meaning of what they have received, teaching them how to appropriate its power and to grow in the new life which is now theirs.

God our Father,
each year You increase the number of Your Church's
    children
who are born in the waters of baptism.
Grant that throughout their lives
Your people may hold fast to the mystery of their new birth
which they have received by faith,
through Him who died for us and rose again
and has given us a share in His victory:
Your only Son, Jesus Christ, our Lord,
who with You and the Holy Spirit
is one God, and who lives and reigns with You for ever.
Amen.[20]

VII
POSTBAPTISMAL
INSTRUCTIONS

Chapter Seventeen

Easter

God has given you a new life of grace and holiness

Last night, my beloved brothers and sisters, during the holy Easter vigil, all the things for which we have been preparing you took place. God gave you a new life, and you put on the spotless garments of grace and holiness. In joy and confidence you made your way to the altar to take part in the heavenly feast prepared for you. The sanctuary was filled with angels watching you come up in procession, hearing you sing your new song, and praising the Lord for the renewal of men and women once stained with sin and now radiant with new life and purity.

Yes, in one single night Mother Church has given birth to a whole generation of new Christians. You have been born again to new life, and have tasted the food and drink of immortality. The bread you received from the altar was the Lord's own Body, and the cup contained His Blood. It was in this wonderful way that the Lord Jesus chose to leave us His Body and Blood to nourish His own life within us; indeed, He has transformed us into the very thing we receive. You have actually become His Body.

In your former life you were like scattered, isolated grains of wheat, until the Lord brought you to His own threshing floor and set His oxen (that is, your teachers and ministers) to toil at the task of threshing you. As catechumens you were winnowed and stored away in the Church's barns; then you gave in your names, and by fasting and exorcisms you were slowly ground into fine flour. After that you were soaked in water and kneaded together into a single loaf. Then you were baked in the fire of the Holy Spirit, to become the Lord's own bread.

In the same way, just as wine is the product of many grapes crushed in the winepress until they become one sweet liquid, so you too have been crushed in the winepress. After the fasts you have endured, after all your labors and humiliations and tears, you have now come in Christ's name to His holy altar to drink from that one cup. Now you belong to our company; we all take that cup together and together we drink from it, because we are all one in the Lord. This is the ultimate aim of sharing the one bread and the one cup, that we should always be one single body, holding fast in undivided charity to one faith, one hope, one mutual love.

I know well that many things have still to be explained. It may strike you as strange that you were not given a complete teaching on the sacraments before you were baptized. However, the ancient discipline of the Church forbids us to reveal the Christian mysteries to the uninitiated. For the full meaning of the sacraments cannot be grasped without the light which they themselves shed in your hearts.

All we did beforehand, therefore, was point out the significance of the rites to make sure you would realize what was happening to you and understand that the sensible signs through which the grace of the sacraments is given to God's people actually contain the reality they symbolize, always provided that we lay hold of this reality by our active faith.

The spiritual interpretation of Scripture

What I want to show you now is that the symbolism of the sacraments is supported by another kind of symbolism. This is something you have not yet been taught. It is the symbolism of the Holy Scriptures—what we call the figurative or typological sense of the Bible. Of course, you are already familiar with the biblical account of the history of our salvation. We spent the earlier weeks of Lent studying the stories of the patriarchs and the wisdom literature. But up till now we have only used those parts of Scripture as a basis for moral teaching on the Christian life. We have not opened up for you the deep, mysterious meaning of the Scriptures, which will help you to understand the sacramental action more fully.

The truth is that there is more than one valid interpretation of scriptural texts. First of all, of course, there is the historical or literal meaning. Then there is the moral lesson which each person can draw from God's word. But over and above these there is a symbolic or mystical sense. All Scripture, we can say, has a literal, a moral, and a spiritual sense.

We have already dwelt sufficiently on the literal and moral senses of Scripture; I now propose to explain the spiritual sense.

It is important to realize that the events of the Old Testament are always a foreshadowing or prefiguration—what we call a *type*—of New Testament realities. The Christian sacraments were actually in existence in God's mind long before the Law of Moses and its ritual observances were promulgated. They were foreshadowed from the beginning of time. God wanted us to know that from the very outset He had a plan to save us and restore us to that loving relationship with Himself that we had lost.

So let us recall the rites of initiation once again, this time discerning all the scriptural types and figures which foreshadowed the grace conferred on you during that holy night. We must not stop short at what our senses convey to us. Saint Paul reminds us to look not at what is visible but at what is invisible, because what can be seen is only transitory; it is the things that are unseen that are permanent (see 2 Cor. 4:18). He also reminds us that everything we can know about God is discernible through the things He has made, and that His eternal power and divinity can be discovered through the things He has done ever since the beginning of the world (Rom. 1:20). Our Lord Himself said the same thing. "Even if you do not believe Me," He told the Jews, "at least believe the things I do" (John 10:38). Now the things God has done are written down for our instruction in Holy Scripture.

The waters of creation

Let us look at the opening words of the Bible. In the beginning, we are told, God created the heavens and the earth. The earth was a formless void; there was darkness over the deep, and God's Spirit hovered over the waters. Then God spoke, and the world came into being; light and darkness, night and day, dry land and sea. God said: "Let the waters bring forth living creatures," and living creatures came to birth. These living creatures were the fish that teemed in the waters of creation.

Do you see that in the very first chapter of the Bible we have a type or figure of Christian baptism? We see the Spirit of God hovering over the primordial waters and cooperating in the work of creation, just as He came down upon the waters of the Jordan when Jesus was baptized and made them the source of His new creation, and just as even now He comes down upon the baptismal waters and makes them bring forth living creatures. The waters of Genesis gave birth to fish; the waters of baptism give birth to human beings. As water gave natural life to those first fishes, so in baptism water gives the new life of grace to you.

You may perhaps know, incidentally, that the early Christians used the symbol of a fish to represent Christ, because the initial letters of the name *Iesous Christos Theou Uios Soter,* Jesus Christ, the Son of God, Savior, made up the Greek word *Ichthus,* which means fish. Anyone drawing the cryptogram of a fish was giving the code sign by which a fellow Christian could recognize him. And surely it is a very appropriate symbol, isn't it, for us who have been reborn in water? Think how freely fish are able to swim through the waves. Storms and tempests may break upon the sea, but fish do not sink because they are in their proper element and swimming is natural to them. The sea for us Christians is the world around us—a stormy sea subject to sudden squalls and violent gales. If we take care to remain in our own proper element like the fish, that is, in the grace of the Lord Jesus whose risen life we share, then we too will be buoyant like the fish, and the rough seas of this world will never drown us.

The flood

Our first prefiguration of baptism, then, is in the waters of creation itself. Now let us take another scriptural type.

In chapter 6 of Genesis we read how the earth God had created grew corrupt in His sight because of men's sins, until at last God declared: "My Spirit shall not remain in man, for he is only flesh" (Gen. 6:3). He decided to bring about a flood to destroy every living thing on the earth; all flesh would perish in the waters of the flood.

Now God's intention was to rid the earth of moral pollution, not to destroy it altogether. So He told Noah to build an ark. When the flood came Noah was to board the ark with all his household, taking with him representatives of all the animals and birds.

The flood lasted forty days, and every living creature was drowned except those on board the ark. When the waters finally began to abate, Noah sent out a raven, which flew off and did not return. Later on Noah sent out a dove, which came back to him that evening with a fresh olive branch in its beak.

You are all familiar with the story. But now I want you to think carefully. Picture the scene: the flood waters, the wooden ark, and the dove. Water, wood, and a dove: the combination of these three things should alert you to the presence of a mystery hidden beneath the surface of this passage.

The water is a type of the water of baptism, in which all flesh is plunged in order to wash away all the sins of the flesh. Every wicked deed that man or woman can commit is drowned and destroyed in that sacramental water. The wood of the ark is a prefiguration of the wood of the Cross to which the Lord Jesus was nailed when He suffered His bitter Passion for us. The dove foreshadows the Holy Spirit, both as He came down upon Jesus in the form of a dove at the river Jordan and as He is sent forth from heaven to bring God's peace to men and women in the baptismal font. As the dove was released from Noah's ark to alight upon a land washed clean by the waters of the flood, so the Holy Spirit comes down upon the soul cleansed from sin by baptism. The raven too has a figurative meaning; it represents the sin which flies away when you are baptized, never to return, provided that you guard your new life and keep yourself clean from sin by obeying God's will.

As early as the time of Noah, then, there was a prefiguring of our baptism. For what was the flood but the means of destroying the corruption of the flesh while preserving one good man, Noah, in order to make him the means of propagating goodness? Surely this is what baptism is. In the font all sins are washed away and grace alone survives. And this, I say, is the reality; what happened in the time of Noah was a mere shadow in comparison with its fulfillment in Jesus Christ and in His Church.

The crossing of the Red Sea

Next we come to the story of the Exodus, which you heard during the paschal vigil. I will not go into detail about the sojourn of the Israelites in Egypt and how they came to be enslaved to Pharaoh. Everyone knows the story, which is clear enough from the historical point of view. Our concern today is to discover the spiritual meaning of this passage of Scripture, for the whole history of the Passover is a type of our salvation through baptism.

When Pharaoh ruthlessly oppressed the Israelites, God sent Moses to bring them out of bondage. Moses instructed the people to sacrifice a lamb and to anoint the doorposts of their houses with its blood, so that the destroying angel might pass over the houses on which he saw this sign. Then he led them out of Egypt. When Moses stretched out his hand over the Red Sea, the Lord made a dry pathway right across it. The waters divided, and the people crossed the sea dryshod, walls of water to right and left. The Egyptians, chasing after them, were engulfed by the sea as it returned to its bed. Every one of Pharaoh's chariots and horsemen was destroyed. That day the Lord delivered Israel from the Egyptians. On reaching the other side, Moses sang a hymn of triumph, while his sister Miriam struck her timbrel and led the women in a dance of exultation. Then the Lord went ahead of the people in a pillar of cloud by day and a pillar of fire by night, to guide them through the desert to the Promised Land.

Now let us turn from the Old Testament to the New, from the type to the reality, and see what all these events signify for us.

First of all, we have Egypt representing the world, Pharaoh and his army representing the devil and all wicked spirits, and the Israelites representing the Christian people.

The Israelites are oppressed by the Egyptians, so God sends Moses into Egypt to lead them out of their bondage to Pharaoh. The human race is enslaved to sin, so God sends Jesus Christ into the world to be their Savior and rescue them from bondage to Satan. The blood of the Passover lamb on their doorposts protects the Israelites from the destroyer; the blood of the unblemished Lamb on the Cross puts demons to flight. Pharaoh pursues the people of Israel as far as the Red Sea; Satan pursues the people of God to the very waters of salvation. Moses divides the sea for the Israelites to pass through; Jesus opens the gates of death and shatters its iron bars. The tyrant of old is drowned in the sea; our tyrant is drowned in the waters of baptism, and our enmity with God destroyed. The people come forth from the sea whole and unscathed; we come up from the font as living from the dead, saved by the grace of Him who called us.

Miriam leads the women, dancing and striking their timbrels, into the desert; the Church leads the baptized, singing hymns and beating their breasts, through the desert of this world into the Promised Land of heaven. A pillar of fire goes ahead of the Israelites to guide them by day, while a pillar of cloud leads them by night. Christ the Lord dispels the shadows of unbelief, sheds the light of truth in human hearts, and says: "Whoever follows Me will not be walking in the dark" (John 8:12). The Holy Spirit comes upon the baptized, and guides all who put their faith in His unseen grace.

From all this you can see that the spiritual meaning of the Old Testament figures is to be found at two levels: first, the victory of Christ on the Cross, through which mankind is set free from sin and death, and then the deliverance granted to each Christian through the sacraments. In the Old Testament God frees an earthly people from an earthly tyrant and leads them out of Egypt into the desert toward the Promised Land. In the New Testament Jesus Christ frees a spiritual people from a spiritual tyrant and leads them out of the world into the Kingdom of God. And in the baptismal font, the Holy Spirit applies this grace to every member of the Church.

Chapter Eighteen

Easter Monday

Further figures of baptism

After our last session, when we saw that there were several prefigurations of baptism in the Books of Genesis and Exodus, I am sure you are all eager to discover the spiritual interpretation of other parts of Scripture. Let us first return to the Book of Exodus to examine the significance of another story about the Israelites on their way from Egypt to the Promised Land.

After they had crossed the Red Sea, the Israelites traveled for three days without finding water. Then they reached a place called Marah, where there was a pool. The people rushed to slake their thirst, but when they tasted the water they found it so bitter as to be undrinkable. Once more they began to grumble and complain. In desperation Moses appealed to the Lord, who told Moses to throw a certain piece of wood into the pool. Moses picked up the stick and threw it into the water. "Try it now," he told the people. Cautiously they sampled it a second time and were amazed to find no trace of bitterness; the water had become wholesome and pleasant to the taste.

This episode is related briefly in the Book of Exodus as an incident in the journey of the Hebrews toward the Promised

Land. However, we now know that the stories we read in the Bible have underlying meanings. In this passage we are meant to find our fourth type of baptism.

The lesson here is that water by itself is incapable of bringing salvation and new life to men. Until it is endowed with the power of the Lord's Cross, it remains on the natural plane. Only when it has been sanctified by the Cross on which our Savior died for us is it fit to be used for sacramental purposes, both in the baptismal font and also in the Eucharist, where, according to the tradition of the Church, it is added to the wine in the chalice.

Inspired by the Holy Spirit, Moses cast wood into the waters of Marah to make them sweet for the people to drink. So also, by the power of the Holy Spirit, the bishop casts the Lord's Cross into the baptismal waters to make them a sweet instrument of divine grace for the Christian people. When does he do this? He does it during the blessing of the font on Holy Saturday, when he traces the sign of the cross three times over the surface of the water, asking God to send His Holy Spirit upon it.

You can understand, then, that it is not enough for us to believe only in what we can see with our bodily eyes, as I said before. What we see with the eyes of the spirit is far more real, far more true, and far more worthy of the acceptance of faith. What the eye sees is already passing away, but the mind perceives eternal mysteries.

The healing of Naaman

Let us turn now to the Second Book of Kings, where we are told the story of Naaman, an important personage at the Syrian court who suffered from a form of leprosy which none of the Syrian doctors was able to cure.

Naaman's wife had a little maidservant who had been

captured in a raid on the neighboring country of Israel. One day this maid remarked to her mistress that there was a prophet in Samaria who could cure Naaman. Naaman reported her statement to the king of Syria, and because the king held Naaman in esteem, he sent him to Israel with money and gifts for the Israelite king, together with a letter of recommendation. "I am sending you my servant Naaman," the letter said, "so that you can cure him of his leprosy." The king of Israel was indignant. "Who does he think I am, to be able to cure lepers?" he demanded. "Can't you see he is trying to pick a quarrel with me, asking me to do impossible things so that he can accuse me?" And he tore his clothes in exasperation.

When the Prophet Elisha heard what had happened, he sent the king a message. "Why have you torn your clothes?" he asked. "Is Israel's God unable to heal a leper? Send the man to me, and he will find out that there is a genuine prophet in Israel."

So Naaman came with his chariot and team of horses and drew up before the door of Elisha's house. But the prophet did no more than send a messenger out to him to tell him to go to the river Jordan and bathe himself seven times in the water, after which the leprosy would disappear. Naaman was not accustomed to being treated so unceremoniously. "Is that all?" he asked. "Have I come all this way merely to be told to bathe in a contemptible river like the Jordan, as if there were not better rivers in Damascus where I could bathe? The prophet might at least have come out and prayed over me and laid his hand on the sore place and healed it."

But his servants, who were devoted to him, pointed out to their master that if the prophet had told him to do something difficult he would not have hesitated. Would it not be a good idea to give Elisha's recommendation a trial, seeing that it was so easy to carry out? Naaman saw the point. He went down to the Jordan, took off his clothes, waded in, and immersed himself seven times over as he had been told. When he came out the seventh time, every trace of the disease had disappeared. His skin was clean and unblemished, like a little child's.

Then Naaman understood that healing does not come from this river or that, but from the Lord, the God of Israel. Returning to Elisha, he gave his testimony: "Now I know that there is no other God except the God of Israel."

What does this story mean for us?

Think once more of what you saw last Saturday night. You saw water and men baptizing. Perhaps you too had thoughts like Naaman's. Perhaps you said to yourselves, "Is this all—this common water and these undistinguished-looking men?"

Yes, my friend, it is all. Indeed it is all; innocence, grace, and holiness are here in all their fullness. You saw everything that human vision could see, but you did not observe the invisible effect of those visible actions. As I keep telling you, the things you cannot see are far greater than the things that meet the eye.

Water by itself has no power to heal. It heals only when it is impregnated with the grace of Jesus Christ. There is a difference between the material element of the sacrament and the spiritual consecration, between the action and its effect. The action is carried out by means of water; it is the Holy Spirit who makes it efficacious. Water does not heal unless the Spirit has first consecrated it.

Yesterday we learned how the baptismal water is purified and sweetened by being signed with Christ's Cross. By that contact with the mystery of our redemption the font is cleansed of every evil influence; then by the invocation of the Holy Spirit it is empowered to give new life to all who are immersed in it.

The slave girl

Let us ask ourselves next who is represented by that little slave girl who spoke to her mistress about the prophet in Israel.

Remember that we have to search out the full meaning hidden in these scriptural texts.

The slave girl is a type of the Church, the Church gathered together from all the nations that were once held captive. I am not speaking of imprisonment to some hostile political power, but of a far worse captivity: slavery to sin and to the tyrannical rule of the devil and his minions. To this captivity the Church herself was once subject, in the sense that before their baptism her members did not yet possess the freedom of God's grace. As through the counsel of the slave girl Naaman was persuaded to seek healing for his leprosy from the prophet in Israel, so through the preaching of the Church unbelievers hear God's prophetic word and are persuaded to seek healing for their sins from their Lord and Savior. Like Naaman, they are at first very doubtful, but when at last they recognize the authority of God's word, they accept baptism and by its grace are cleansed of all their guilt. They come up from the water unblemished, like newborn children.

Faith in the power of the Spirit

Naaman refused to believe at first, but that was before he was healed. You, on the contrary, are already healed, so can have no excuse for doubting now. That is why I warned you not to give credence only to what you can see with your bodily eyes. If your faith were only in visible things, you might well react as Naaman did. You might shrug your shoulders and say: "Is this the great mystery I have been told about? Is this the blessing that no eye has seen, nor ear heard, nor the heart of man conceived? All I can see is water, ordinary water such as I wash with every day. How often have I taken a bath without being any holier for it! How is this water going to cleanse me from my guilt?"

I repeat and insist, water cannot purify anyone without the Holy Spirit. Scripture tells us there is a triple witness in baptism:

water, blood, and Spirit. Water for man's cleansing, blood for his ransoming, Spirit for raising him to life. These three witnesses are one. Take any one of them away, and there is no longer any sacrament. Without the Cross of Christ and the blood of His Passion, water is nothing but a common element without any sacramental effect. Without water there is no rebirth, because Jesus said that unless a man is born again of water and the Holy Spirit, he cannot enter the Kingdom of God. And without the presence of the Holy Spirit, there is no grace.

Even an unbaptized catechumen believes in the Cross of the Lord Jesus. He has been told how Jesus was crucified for his salvation, and he was marked with the sign of the cross on his forehead the day he became a catechumen. But until he is baptized in the name of the Father, the Son, and the Holy Spirit, he cannot obtain forgiveness nor a share in the life of grace.

Naaman lived in the time of the Old Testament. On becoming a believer he submitted to the Law of Moses, and it was into the old Law that he was baptized, immersing himself seven times. But when you were baptized into the death of Christ, you immersed yourself three times in the name of the Most Holy Trinity. Remember how you declared your faith in the Father, in the Son, and in the Holy Spirit, and how you were plunged in the water after you answered each of the interrogations. When you made that profession of faith, you died to the world and rose to life in God.

Believe me then, my friends, this is no ordinary water. It is the vehicle of power beyond all telling.

Chapter Nineteen

Easter Tuesday

The baptism of Jesus

We have seen that Christian baptism was prefigured in many of the events recorded in the Old Testament. Now we can look at the Gospels and find that images of baptism are present there as well.

First of all, the form of the Christian baptismal rite can be discerned in the baptism of Jesus Himself. As John was baptizing the people in the river Jordan, Jesus came to him and asked to be baptized. John objected: "Are You asking to be baptized by me? It should be the other way round; I am the one who needs to be baptized by You." But Jesus replied: "Let it be this way. It is right for us to meet all the demands of the law and everything that God's justice requires" (Matt. 3:13–15).

According to the Lord's own words, then, by being baptized we meet all the demands of the law and the justice of God. Just as Naaman was cleansed of leprosy by washing in the Jordan, so by being baptized in that same river Jesus fulfilled all that was prescribed in the Law of Moses. And so it is with us: we are cleansed of all our sins by being baptized in the water which Jesus consecrated at His own baptism.

Why do you think Jesus went down into the river? Was He polluted by guilt that needed to be washed away? Indeed not; Scripture tells us He committed no sin. But He had identified Himself with us. He had taken our human flesh, and that flesh was in need of purification. Baptismal cleansing was not necessary for Him, but it is necessary for us, who remain subject to sin. He did not come to be baptized in order to be reborn and sanctified in the water, as the rest of us do. He came rather, in company with the Holy Spirit, to sanctify the water Himself.

Jesus gave His redemptive power to the element of water, consecrating it for sacramental use. By His own baptism in the Jordan He instituted the saving rite by which we are cleansed of sin. He went down into the water and, as John baptized Him, the Holy Spirit descended in the form of a dove. Then a voice came from heaven, saying, "This is My beloved Son, with whom I am well pleased."

So then, we have this solemn scene in the Gospel: Jesus goes down into the water, the Holy Spirit descends in the form of a dove, and the Father speaks from heaven. Does it not strike you that there at the Jordan, where Christian baptism was instituted, we have the presence of the blessed Trinity, Father, Son, and Holy Spirit?

The healing of the paralytic

Now let us turn to another part of the Gospel. In the passage from Saint John which was read at the eucharistic liturgy we heard the story of the paralyzed man healed in the pool of Bethesda in Jerusalem. We are told that an angel used to go down into this pool at certain times and stir up the water, and that the first person who stepped into the pool after the disturbance would be healed of whatever disease he was suffering from (John 5:1–15). One person each year was cured in this way, but only at the moment when the angel had come down and stirred the water. Ordinarily the pool had no healing properties.

Now this pool gives us another image of Christian baptism. But it also provides us with a further illustration of the great difference between the image and the reality. The water at Bethesda was stirred only occasionally and in this one place, whereas the baptismal waters of the Church are continually active everywhere. The water of the pool only healed the body; baptism heals both body and soul. The one delivers the body from sickness; the other delivers both body and soul from sin. The water of the pool cured only one person each year; the grace of Christian baptism flows daily, increases daily, superabounds daily. It flows through kingdoms, peoples, nations; countless men and women rejoice in its gift. In the sacrament of baptism God gives the Church a far more generous fund of grace than He gave to the pool of Bethesda, where a whole crowd of sick people continued to lie because only one a year could be healed. No one lies unhealed beside the Christian font; whoever desires to be whole and to receive new life comes to be baptized and is cured. The water is always ready to heal, as soon as anyone comes. Only those who refuse to come remain sick.

At Bethesda the stirring of the water was the signal that the angel had come. Because of the weakness of their faith, those people needed a visible sign. But you are asked to believe that the Holy Spirit, not an angel, descended into the font last Saturday. You will not have seen any visible movement of the water. Signs like that are for people who do not yet believe, whereas faith is demanded from Christians.

In the Bible we are told that the Lord sent visible fire from heaven to prove that Yahweh was the true God and Elijah His prophet (1 Kings 18:38). For us who believe in the true God and in Jesus Christ whom He has sent into the world, the action of the Holy Spirit is invisible. He is indeed a consuming fire, coming down from heaven upon those who receive the sacramental gifts and making them an acceptable sacrifice to the Lord; but He calls Christians to a greater and more mature faith by concealing His action from their senses.

Now the angel who descended was a figure or type of our Lord Jesus Christ. According to the Gospel the angel went down into the pool "at a certain time." The figurative meaning of this is that the Lord Jesus reserved His coming until the time specified by His Father, the time that Scripture calls "the last hour." Mankind had waited long ages for His coming; it was the evening of the world when at last He came on earth to arrest its decline and prevent its total eclipse.

There is a meaning to be found in every detail of the story. Our Lord Jesus Christ comes to the pool and sees the crowds of sick people lying there waiting to be helped into the water. Since only one can be healed, the sick lie near the edge of the pool. When the water stirs, what a stampede there is to get in before the others. Attendants rush to their patients; everyone shoves and elbows his way forward, often endangering the lives of his neighbors. Jesus, however, picks out a paralyzed man who has been lying there for thirty-eight years, and tells him to step into the water. The invalid explains that he has no one to help him, and so someone else always gets there first. His actual words are, "I have no man to put me into the pool when the water stirs."

"I have no man," he said. And so he lay there year after year, unable to receive healing. He did not know that the Man he was waiting for was Jesus Christ, God made man. Only through Jesus, born for us of the Virgin Mary, can anyone be saved. After the Incarnation people are no longer healed one at a time by some pale foreshadowing of divine power; the living reality prefigured by these cures heals everyone who puts his faith in Jesus. Baptism derives its power from the death on the Cross of Jesus Christ, the Son of God. He is the Man who lifts us up with Himself on the Cross and carries us to the waters of healing and rebirth. Jesus Christ is the man for whom the whole world waits, the mediator between God and man.

The healing of the man born blind

Another great figure of baptism appears in the Gospel of Saint John. Writing long after the other evangelists, he saw more deeply than they into the theological meaning of the events he was recording. He saw all Christ's actions as mysterious signs, and we shall not be deceived if we look at his descriptions of them for an underlying significance. Matthew, Mark, and Luke all describe the cure of the blind men, but only John reports that Jesus spat on the ground and made clay, applied it to the eyes of a man who had been blind from birth, and told him to wash it off in the pool called Siloam. John tells us that the blind man went off and bathed his eyes; when he came back he was able to see (John 9).

You may remember that we heard this passage of the Gospel read at the eucharistic liturgy on the third Sunday of Lent. Like all the readings for this sacred season, it was chosen because of its teaching on baptism.

Now I want each one of you to think of himself as that blind man. Consider the eyes of your spirit, how blind they were at one time to the things of God and to the new life offered in the sacraments, how you could see only the outward signs and not the inward reality. Then one day you met Jesus. He took clay and applied it to your eyes. When was that? you ask. It was the day you gave in your name as a candidate for baptism and joined the class of learners. That was the beginning of the whole process of your enlightenment. You learned to recognize all that was wrong in your life, to repent of your sins and confess them, acknowledging the condition in which all of us are born blind to the light of God's grace.

You must not imagine baptism can ever be unnecessary. I

remember telling one man that at his age it was high time he was baptized. "Why should I be baptized?" he objected. "I haven't committed any very great sins, have I?" This man had not yet had clay applied to his eyes; that is, Jesus had not opened his eyes to see the real state of his soul. There is absolutely no man without sin. Anyone who is looking for the salvation Jesus offers us in baptism is simply acknowledging that he is human, in need of forgiveness.

The clay Jesus applied to your eyes was the grace to recognize your sins and be sorry for them. It was the grace to realize your need for a savior. When you had fully understood your own weakness and inability to help yourself, He said to you: "Go and wash in the pool at Siloam."

Saint John explains that the name Siloam means "Sent." Jesus Christ was the one sent by the Father into the world to set us free through the power of His Cross and Resurrection. The Lord was telling you to go and wash in the baptismal font, upon which the sign of His saving Cross is traced and over which His death and Resurrection are proclaimed; to go to the living spring of water in which Jesus has redeemed every human being and washed away every sin.

And so you went to the pool and washed, and came back able to see. On the holy night of Easter you went to the baptistery and washed in the sacred font; then you came to the altar of God and began to see things you had never seen before. Through the waters of baptism and the proclamation of the Lord's Cross and Resurrection, your eyes were opened, so that you, who beforehand were so blind of heart, could now see the true light of these sacramental mysteries.

Chapter Twenty

Easter Wednesday

The transformation of human nature

We have seen baptism prefigured in the creation, in the flood, in the crossing of the Red Sea, in the pillars of light and cloud, in the waters of Marah, in the healing of Naaman, in the cure of the paralytic, and in the healing of the man born blind.

Now let us consider the meaning of the white garments you were given after you came up from the font.

These white garments, as I said before, are a sign of your new life of purity. How often we repeat those words which David prayed in the psalm, "Lord, sprinkle me with hyssop and I shall be clean. Wash me, and I shall become whiter than snow" (Ps. 51:7). Whiter than snow! Is it possible? Yes, because the snow's whiteness is soon spoiled, but nothing can spoil the grace you have received, so long as you hold fast to it.

There is a reference in the text I have just quoted to the Law, the Prophets, and the Gospel. In the old Law Moses used a bunch of hyssop to sprinkle the blood of the sacrificial lamb over the people for the atonement of their guilt. In the prophecy of Isaiah the Lord declares, "Though your sins are as scarlet, I will make them white as snow" (Is. 1:18). And the Gospel tells us that Jesus' clothing became white as snow at the Transfiguration, as He showed His disciples a brief glimpse of the glory of His resurrection life.

All these words of Scripture have been fulfilled in you. You have been washed clean of all your sins and have put on the white garments of a new and radiant life of holiness, the risen life of the Lord Jesus, the life by which the whole Church now lives as His Bride. It is the Church, the Bride, who has received these white garments "by means of the cleansing water of rebirth" (Titus 3:5), and it is the Church who says of herself in the Song of Songs: "I am dark of skin, but beautiful, daughters of Jerusalem" (Song 1:5); dark through the frailty of her human condition, beautiful through God's grace; dark because she consists of sinners, beautiful because she has put her faith in the Lord and has been transformed in the sacrament of baptism.

The daughters of Jerusalem represent the angels. They see all these white garments here and ask each other in amazement: "Who is this coming up from the desert, all in shining white?" (Song 8:5, following the Septuagint). "Previously she was only a swarthy desert-dweller, but look at her now! How has this sudden transformation come about?"

Yes, it is a marvel in the sight of the angels to see human nature clothed in such loveliness, to see what was previously stained and tarnished suddenly shining bright before them. Our human nature is so much lower than the angels' that their faith was put to a great test when God's Son stooped down to become one of us. Saint Peter says things have been bestowed on us which even the angels long to see (1 Pet. 1:12). The mystery of God's plan had not been fully disclosed to the angels from the beginning; consequently, when they saw Jesus rising from the dead and our flesh and blood ascending into heaven, they could not comprehend it.

But the Lord Jesus loves His Church. He gave Himself up

for her. For her sake He put on filthy garments, as we read in the prophecy of Zechariah (Zech. 3:3). In other words, He took our sinful condition upon Himself and shared our degradation. Now He sees His Bride dressed in spotless white, and exclaims: "How beautiful you are, my love, how beautiful you are!" (Song 4:1).

The interpretation of the Song of Songs

In interpreting Scripture, we can apply many texts to both the Church and the individual soul. Solomon's marriage song can be read as an expression of God's love for His Church, but it is also a figure of the sacramental union between Christ and the Christian soul. So when you hear the words, "How beautiful you are, my love!" you will not be wrong in understanding them as addressed by Jesus Christ to each one of you as you come up from the font, washed clean in the waters of rebirth.

The Bridegroom in the Song of Songs describes the Bride's appearance in a series of poetic images. "Your teeth," he says, "are like a flock of shorn ewes as they come up from the washing. All of them bear twins, and there is not a barren one among them. Your lips are a scarlet thread" (Song 4:1–3). In these verses the Church is represented as a flock of sheep that have been shorn and relieved of their superfluous fleece, because she is rich with the many virtues of all those who have come from the washing (that is, from the font), where they have been disencumbered of all their sins. That they all bear twins means that the newly baptized bring to the Lord their double offering of faith in His saving mystery and of the good deeds His grace enables them to perform. Their lips, like a scarlet thread, sing the praises of the Cross and of the blood shed for them by the Lord Jesus.

In her newborn children the Church is beautiful, and the Word of God says to her: "You are wholly beautiful, my love, without a single blemish," because all her guilt has been wiped away in the baptismal waters. "Come from Lebanon, my promised bride, come from Lebanon" (Song 4:8). The Church has renounced the world and put her faith in her Savior; she has celebrated her Passover from this life and has come to Christ, the Word of God, who once again lovingly assures her: "How beautiful you are, how lovely, my love, my delight!" (Song 7:7).

Then the Church responds to her Lord, calling Him her brother, and expressing her longing to embrace Him. "I will lead you," she declares, "into my mother's house, and there you shall teach me" (Song 8:1, 2). The meaning of this text is that the Church finds such joy in the gifts of God's grace that she longs to enter into the fullness of the mysteries He has hidden in the sacraments and to consecrate herself wholly to Christ. Though she has indeed found Him, she cannot be satisfied until she is wholly one with Him. Knowing she can never love Him enough, she continually strives to increase her love, and at the same time begs the daughters of Jerusalem to rouse Him to greater love for her. Here the daughters of Jerusalem are the faithful members of the Church, through whose holy lives she receives even greater tokens of the Lord's love for her.

To such loving desires, to such beauty and grace—for no stain of sin remains in those who are baptized—the Lord Jesus is swift to respond. "Set me like a seal upon your heart, like a seal upon your arm" (Song 8:6), He says to her. "You are wholly beautiful, my dearest love; there is nothing wanting to your loveliness. Set me as a seal upon your heart; let your faith be enlightened by the completion and perfecting of these sacraments of initiation. Let your good deeds shine out, so that all the world may see that you have been created anew in God's likeness. Let no persecution ever weaken your love; for that love no flood can quench, no torrents drown" (see Song 8:7).

The royal priesthood of the faithful

How do we set the Lord Jesus as a seal upon our hearts? Let me explain.

In the font you died with Christ and were born again to new life. But that new life still had to be perfected; the grace and energy already implanted in your soul at baptism needed to be brought into action. The sacrament of baptism, in other words, needed to be completed by the sacrament of chrismation.

You remember that after you came up from the font you knelt before the bishop, who anointed your head with chrism.[21] Now this anointing must first be seen in connection with the priestly anointing of the Old Testament. It is described in Leviticus 21, where the text says that the high priest on whose head chrism is poured is preeminent over his brothers; he bears on his person the consecration of his God, given to him by the oil of anointing (Lev. 21:12).

Chrism, as you know, is made of oil blended with certain perfumes. The recipe for it is given in the Book of Exodus (Ex. 30:22–25). It was with this perfumed oil that Moses anointed his brother Aaron when he ordained him to the high priesthood at God's command. (Notice that Aaron had previously bathed himself in water.) There is a reference to this in the Psalms, where David speaks of the life of the Christian community as being like the "oil poured out on Aaron's head and running down his beard upon the collar of his robe" (Ps. 133:3).

You can see from this that the postbaptismal anointing consecrates you to a share in the priesthood of the faithful. The whole body of the Church is anointed to exercise a priestly function, to offer a spiritual sacrifice of praise, just as Saint Peter tells us in his first letter. "You are a chosen race," he says, "a royal priesthood, a consecrated nation, a people set apart to sing the praises of God, who called you out of darkness into His wonderful light" (1 Pet. 2:9).

Notice that Saint Peter calls us a *royal* priesthood. Not only the high priest, but also the king of Israel received an anointing with chrism. Saul and David were anointed by Samuel; Solomon was anointed by Zadok the priest (again, notice, after he had bathed in the Gihon). All of you, too, have been anointed by the Holy Spirit to share in the Kingdom of God as well as in the priesthood of the faithful.

Both high priest and king were referred to as "the Lord's Anointed": in Greek, *Christos,* in Latin, *Christus,* from the word *chrism.* Jesus Himself was given the name Christ because He was anointed with the Holy Spirit by God the Father at the time of His baptism in the Jordan. The first Christians in the Acts of the Apostles speak of Him as "your holy servant Jesus, whom you anointed" (Acts 4:27), and Saint Peter proclaims "Jesus of Nazareth, whom God anointed with the Holy Spirit" (Acts 10:38). And now that you have been baptized into Christ and have put on Christ, you too have become the Lord's anointed by receiving the sign of the Holy Spirit. Just as Christ was crucified, buried, and raised to life in the flesh, and you have been crucified, buried, and raised to life with Him symbolically in baptism, so too Christ was anointed with the oil of gladness because He is the source of spiritual joy, and you have been anointed with chrism because you are His members.

The seal of the Spirit

This final anointing, together with the laying on of hands, constitutes the sacrament of chrismation. In this sacrament you received the seal of the Holy Spirit to complete and perfect the work begun in you when you were born to new life in the font. The bishop laid his hands on your head and prayed that the almighty God and Father of our Lord Jesus Christ, who had already given you new birth in water and the Holy Spirit, would now send the Advocate upon you and give you the spirit of wisdom and understanding, the spirit of counsel and fortitude, the spirit of knowledge and piety, the spirit of reverent fear. And then he made the sign of the cross on your forehead with chrism, sealing you with the seal of the Spirit. This is the seal we heard about in the reading from Saint Paul's letter to the Corinthians, where he says: "It is God Himself who assures us that we are in Christ. He has anointed us, marking us with His seal and giving us the pledge of the Spirit that we carry in our hearts" (2 Cor. 1:21, 22).

The Spirit's sevenfold gifts

Never forget that you have received the seal of the Holy Spirit and His sevenfold gifts, and guard carefully what you have received. God the Father has sealed you, Christ the Lord has chrismated you, and He has given you the pledge of His Spirit. All virtues and spiritual gifts are given by the Spirit, and when you are chrismated you receive the power to exercise them all. But the seven named specifically in the bishop's prayer are known as the seven gifts of the Holy Spirit, because they are, as it were, the basic or cardinal virtues. After all, what could be more fundamental than that spirit of loving sonship that we call piety, more important than the knowledge of God and the counsel which is His guidance, more necessary than fortitude and reverence for God? To be afraid of the world is weakness, but to fear God and none but Him is to possess the key to true strength. These gifts you received when you were chrismated, because, in the words of Saint Paul to the Ephesians (3:10), the wisdom of God has many ways of expressing itself. So too the Holy Spirit is manifold and comprehensive, pouring out upon us every gift we need.

Keep your anointing unspotted. If it abides in you, it will teach you everything. We have this assurance from Scripture, where Saint John says: "The anointing you received from Him abides in you, so that you have no need of anyone to teach you; His anointing teaches you all things. As it has taught you, abide in him" (1 John 2:27).

Chapter Twenty-one

Easter Thursday

The Eucharist

We have discussed the sacraments of baptism and chrismation; today, I would like to consider the other sacrament you received on Holy Saturday—the Eucharist. How often you must have read or heard the account of the Last Supper without realizing the connection between what took place in the upper room and what takes place on our altars. You did not know that Christians received the Lord's Body and Blood in the Holy Eucharist.

Jesus has told us, "My flesh is real food and My blood is real drink. Unless you eat My flesh and drink My blood you cannot dwell in Me, nor can you have eternal life" (see John 6:53–56). When He first spoke in this way, people objected: "How can this man give us His flesh to eat?" Even the Lord's disciples could not accept His teaching on this subject, and many of them withdrew from His company in horror. He did not try to stop them, but He asked the Twelve if they too intended to leave Him. Peter's reply was, "How can we leave You? To whom should we go? You have the words of eternal life" (John 6:38).

For us, too, no other reply is possible. We too must put our faith in the Lord's words. You may be tempted to say: "All I can see on the altar is bread—ordinary, everyday bread that the people brought from their homes for the offering. Are you telling me it is now the Body of Christ?"

Yes, that is exactly what I am telling you. It was ordinary everyday bread before the words of Christ were pronounced over it. As soon as they were uttered, it became the Body of Christ. As Saint Paul teaches us, on the night that the Lord Jesus was betrayed He took bread, and, giving thanks, He broke it and handed it to His disciples, saying: "Take and eat. This is My body." And, taking the cup, He again gave thanks and said: "Take and drink. This is My blood" (1 Cor. 11:23–25). Jesus makes this statement in clear and unambiguous language; how can anyone presume to dispute it?

The word of Elijah had power to bring down fire from heaven; will not the word of Christ have power to change the nature of bread and wine? The sacrament you receive from the altar has been consecrated by the words of Christ Himself. The words of institution are the actual words spoken by the Lord at the Last Supper. All the earlier parts of the eucharistic liturgy— the praise we offer to God, the prayers the priest says for the people—all these are words of human origin; but when it comes to the consecration of the blessed sacrament, the priest no longer uses his own words, but Christ's. The bread and wine are changed into the Body and Blood of Christ, therefore, by the word of Christ Himself, the word by which all things were made.

Scripture tells us that the Lord spoke His word and the heavens were made; He spoke His word and the earth was made; He spoke His word and the seas were made; He spoke His word and every created thing came into existence. Jesus Christ is the Lord by whose word the whole universe was created. And if the word of the Lord Jesus has the power to create things out of nothing, surely it has the power to change existing things into something else. Before baptism you yourself belonged to the old creation, but once you were consecrated to God in the font, you became a new creature. When He so desires, Christ can change anything in creation and the laws of nature themselves, simply by His word.

The consecration of bread and wine

I want you to be absolutely sure of this teaching, to be convinced that the conversion of bread and wine into the Lord's Body and Blood is effected by words that are divine in origin. Listen carefully while I repeat what the priest says:

> FATHER, APPROVE OUR OFFERING,
> MAKE IT ACCEPTABLE TO YOU,
> AN OFFERING IN SPIRIT AND IN TRUTH,
> FOR IT IS THE SACRAMENTAL SIGN[22]
> OF THE BODY AND BLOOD OF OUR LORD JESUS CHRIST,
> WHO, THE DAY BEFORE HE SUFFERED,
> TOOK BREAD IN HIS SACRED HANDS
> AND, LOOKING UP TO HEAVEN,
> TO YOU, HOLY FATHER, ALMIGHTY AND ETERNAL GOD,
> GAVE YOU THANKS AND PRAISE,
> BROKE THE BREAD,
> GAVE IT TO HIS APOSTLES AND DISCIPLES AND SAID:
> TAKE THIS, ALL OF YOU, AND EAT IT.
> THIS IS MY BODY WHICH WILL BE BROKEN FOR ALL MANKIND.

Through these words the bread is consecrated. Now listen to the second part:

> IN THE SAME WAY,
> AT THE END OF SUPPER ON THE EVE OF HIS PASSION,
> HE TOOK THE CUP,
> AND, RAISING HIS EYES TO YOU,

HOLY FATHER, ALMIGHTY AND ETERNAL GOD,
AGAIN HE GAVE YOU THANKS AND PRAISE,
GAVE THE CUP TO HIS APOSTLES AND DISCIPLES AND SAID:
TAKE THIS, ALL OF YOU, AND DRINK FROM IT.
THIS IS MY BLOOD.

Notice that whether the narrative refers to Christ's Body or to His Blood, the priest employs the evangelist's words until he reaches the point where it says *Take this.* From then on he repeats Christ's own words: "Take this, all of you, and eat it: this is My Body," or, "Take this, all of you, and drink from it: this is My Blood." Note the exact wording: *The day before He suffered, He took bread in His sacred hands.* He took *bread,* notice; the bread is not yet consecrated. But now come the actual words of Christ: *Take this, all of you, and eat it: this is My Body.* Once these words are pronounced, the bread has become Christ's Body. Again, before Christ's words, the chalice contains wine and water. The moment His all-powerful words are pronounced, they come into effect; the wine and water become the Blood which redeemed the world.

The Christian priesthood

We believe that what Christ our Lord did on earth by offering Himself in sacrifice for us all, He continues to do in heaven as our true High Priest. And in order that the one sacrifice of His may continue to be offered on earth, He chooses certain members of His Church to be priests of the New Covenant. The Holy Spirit comes down upon them to empower and ordain them. They do not offer new sacrifices, like the repeated immolations of animal victims which the Mosaic Law prescribed. They continue to offer one and the same sacrifice in every place throughout the world until the end of time, because there is only one sacrifice that was offered for us all, the sacrifice of Jesus

Christ our Lord, who suffered death on the Cross for our sake. "By a single offering," says Scripture, "He has perfected His work for all time in those who are sanctified" (Heb. 10:14).

So at all times and in all places Christians continue to celebrate the commemoration of this one sacrifice.

Do not ask yourselves whether the priests deserve to have their prayers answered. God answers them not because they are holy men, but because of the office of the priesthood which is His own gift and which He has pledged Himself to honor. They are the successors of the Holy Apostles, who received the power of Holy Orders from the Lord Jesus and handed it on to us. Have faith that Jesus will honor the prayers of His own priests. Did He not assure us that where two or three are gathered together, there He would be in their midst? Surely, then, we can be all the more certain of His presence where the Church is assembled to celebrate the sacred mysteries.

The privilege of communicating in the sacred mysteries belongs to all the baptized without exception. However, a greater measure of grace is received by the person who communicates more worthily, that is, the person who lives a life of deeper faith and love, for of course no one can be truly worthy of such a gift. We are still mortal and liable to fall into sin; how could we be worthy to receive the immortal and incorruptible Body of Christ, who is in heaven at the Father's right hand? Nevertheless, we trust in the mercy of the Lord, who desires to give us these gifts. We come forward to receive them with all the faith and love we can muster, in order to be as worthy as human nature permits.

A gift more precious than gold

When you come to receive Holy Communion, then, do not come with your arm stretched out or your fingers parted. Make your left hand into a throne for your right, because your right hand is about to welcome your King. Shape your palm into a cup, and so receive the Body of Christ our Lord, to whom all authority has been given in heaven and on earth.

The priest will hold up the host and say to you:

THE BODY OF CHRIST.

You reply:

AMEN.

By this short word you mean: Yes, it is true. I believe and proclaim that this is truly Christ's Body I am receiving; this is truly the reality that was foreshadowed in the Old Testament. Very reverently touch your eyes with His most sacred Body, and then consume it, being very careful not to drop any particle of it. Imagine how carefully you would guard gold dust if it were given you, making sure you did not lose any part of it. And is not the Lord's Body more precious than gold? Even greater care should be taken, then, not to lose the least fragment of this most blessed sacrament.

After this, go to receive the Blood of Christ from the chalice. Do not reach out for it, but bow your head in homage, say *Amen,* and then, with great reverence and love, drink from the Lord's cup. While His Blood is still on your lips, touch it with your hand and bless your eyes, your brow, and your other senses.

Christ our Lord is now within you. Praise and thank Him with all your heart, and join with all the congregation in thanksgiving, for we have all received this spiritual food together and it is right that we should give thanks in common.

Do not allow the faults that arise from human weakness to keep you from Holy Communion. We must not of course receive the Lord's Body and Blood carelessly, sinning without scruple; if we do that we are condemning ourselves. But if we have our salvation at heart and are eager to do what is good, our sins of frailty will do us no harm. On the contrary, we shall be strengthened by receiving Holy Communion, and the grace which this sacrament confers will help us to do good works and wipe out our faults, provided they are not grave and deliberate, and that we repent of them and ask God's forgiveness.

The sacrament of reconciliation

If we have committed a serious sin of any kind which implies rejection of God's will, we must abstain from communion. But we must not allow ourselves to stay away indefinitely. No indeed; we must rouse ourselves to repentance. We must not leave the healing of such sins to themselves. God has given us the remedy of confession, according to the discipline of the Church. This is the treatment of sins that God has entrusted to the priests of the Church, who are trained to use it with great care, adjusting the treatment they give to penitents according to the gravity of their sins. For this reason we should approach priests with great confidence, and reveal our sins to them. They will treat us with loving compassion, never making public anything we tell them. In this way we shall be able to put our lives in order and correct our faults, and so be free to receive the precious gifts to which we are invited.

Chapter Twenty-two

Easter Friday

Scriptural types of the Eucharist

In discussing the sacraments of baptism and chrismation, we examined the ways in which they were prefigured by events in the Old Testament. Now that we are considering the Eucharist, I would like to show you some of the scriptural types of this sacrament too.

Melchizedek

You remember the story in the fourteenth chapter of Genesis: how the kings joined battle in the valley of Siddim, which is now the Dead Sea, and the conquerors carried off all the possessions of the people of Sodom and Gomorrah, including Abraham's nephew Lot and all he owned. When Abraham was told of this, he mustered his men and rode off in pursuit. He defeated the raiders and recaptured the spoils, together with his nephew and all the other prisoners. On his way back, he was met by Melchizedek, a priest of the Most High God, who brought gifts of bread and wine which Abraham received with great reverence.

Notice that it was not Abraham but Melchizedek who

offered the bread and wine. The Letter to the Hebrews points out that Scripture represents Melchizedek as having neither father nor mother. There is no mention of his ancestry, nor is there any indication of his beginning or end. He is like the Son of God and, like Him, remains a priest for ever. His name means "King of Righteousness, King of Peace" (Heb. 7:2, 3).

Now I ask you: Is it possible for a mere man to be the King of Righteousness or the King of Peace, especially a man living in those primitive and violent times? Hardly. Scripture describes Melchizedek in these mysterious terms because he is a type or figure of our Lord Jesus Christ, who is the righteousness of God, the wisdom of God (see 1 Cor. 1:24, 30), and the peace of God— Jesus who said to His Apostles, "My peace I give you, My peace I leave with you" (John 14:27). Jesus Christ is the One who in His divine nature has no mother. He shares His being with God the Father, whose only Son He is. And in His human nature He has no father, because He was born of a virgin by the power of the Holy Spirit. He has no beginning and no end, because He Himself is the beginning and the end of all things, the Alpha and Omega, the first and the last (Rev. 21:6). You see then how Melchizedek was like the Son of God in all things, including the priesthood, for Scripture says of Christ, "You are a priest for ever of the order of Melchizedek" (Heb. 7:17; Ps. 110:4).

All this shows that the bread and wine which you receive in the Christian mysteries are not the mere offerings of men. They are a divine gift, brought by the Son of God, who was prefigured by Melchizedek and who Himself blessed Abraham, our father in the faith. In Abraham He blessed all of us who believe in His name.

The manna and the rock

We have seen that baptism was prefigured in the account of the Exodus. Now I want to show you how that story also contains an image of the Lord's Supper and our communion in the sacred mysteries. But let me warn you not to expect an exact correspondence in every detail of the story; the reality always surpasses the figure. Bearing that in mind, listen to Saint Paul:

> I want you to understand that our forefathers were all under the cloud and all of them passed through the Red Sea, and so they were all baptized into the fellowship of Moses in the cloud and in the sea. They all ate the same supernatural food and drank the same supernatural drink, because they all drank from the supernatural rock that accompanied them in the desert, and that rock was Christ (1 Cor. 10:1–3).

They all ate the same supernatural food, he says. Just as, after their passage through the Red Sea, the Israelites came to a new and marvelous feast—the manna—so after passing through the water of the font you came up to the altar; and just as they found a wonderful kind of drink in the desert where there was neither spring nor running stream—water flowing abundantly from a barren rock—so you were given a mysterious drink, the blood of our salvation.

Not only are the Christian sacraments more ancient than those of the Old Testament, but they are also far more noble and precious. In saying this I have no intention of belittling the miracle God worked for the Israelites in raining down manna for them. It was indeed one of the great marvels of His love and power. He gave the people food from on high every day without their having to work for it—the bread of angels, Scripture calls it. It was all part of His will and purpose for them, just as the sacraments of the New Covenant are His will and purpose for us (see Luke 7:30).

But the fact remains that all those who ate the manna died in the desert, whereas the sacramental food you have received is the living bread that comes down from heaven, the staple of eternal life. Whoever eats this bread, Jesus told His disciples, will never die, because it is the living Body of Christ (John 6:51).

I ask you then: which is of greater value, the bread of angels or the Body of Christ, the Body of Life itself? The manna came down from heaven, but the living bread of the Eucharist comes to you from the Maker of the heavens. Manna was the bread of angels, the Eucharist is the Body of the Lord of angels. Manna would not keep fresh for more than one day, whereas the Body of Christ is immune to decay; whoever eats it in reverent faith will share its incorruptible nature.

For the Israelites water flowed from a rock in the desert, but for you blood flows from the wounds of Christ. That water satisfied the Israelites for a short time, but the blood Christ pours out for you is a cleansing spring that never dries up. The Israelites were soon thirsty again, but you who drink the Blood of Christ will never thirst any more.

The miracles God worked by raining down manna and making water flow from the rock were types foreshadowing the reality which you receive in the Eucharist. Marvelous though these types and figures were, the things they foreshadowed are more wonderful still. Beyond all question the light is greater than the shadow, the reality greater than the figure, the Body of the Author and Giver of life greater than manna falling from the sky.

The Lord is your Shepherd

Those are two scriptural types of the Eucharist, but I do not have enough time now to examine all the others. As we have only one more day together, I shall not linger over them, but I suggest you read the Scriptures yourselves with your newly enlightened eyes and see what depths of spiritual meaning you can discover in them. Now that you know about the sacraments God planned for us in His wisdom so long ago, you will find reminders of them in passages which you formerly understood only in their literal sense.

How often, for instance, you must have heard the twenty-third psalm without realizing that it finds its full meaning in the sacraments of the Church! For in this psalm—the very song you yourselves sang on Saturday night when you came up to the Lord's Table for the first time—all the sacraments you have received can be discerned. It expresses the confidence and trust of the newly baptized and their gratitude for their new life.

Let us recite it together now, and as we do so it will all become clear to you.

> The Lord is my shepherd; there is nothing I shall want.
> He gives me a place of rest in green pastures
> and leads me out by peaceful waters,
> where He renews my life within me.
> He guides me along the right path
> for the sake of His name.
> Even if I walk in the shadow of death
> I fear no evil,
> because You are with me.
> Your crook and Your staff give me comfort and protection.
> You have prepared a table for me,
> to strengthen me against my enemies.
> My head You have anointed with oil,
> and how glorious is the blessing-cup You offer me!
> Your love and mercy pursue me all my days,
> and I shall live in the Lord's house
> my whole life long.

The Lord Jesus Christ is your shepherd. He has called you to become a member of His flock, that is, His Church, which lacks no blessing. You will want for nothing, because anyone who eats the eucharistic bread will never know hunger again. He gives you a place of rest in green pastures (the fields of Paradise from which you had strayed), leading you out of exile by means of the waters of baptism. In those peaceful waters He takes away your burden of sin and gives you new life.

The Good Shepherd guides you along the right path; indeed He Himself is the Way. In baptism you die with Him, but since you die in symbol or, as it were, in shadow, you have nothing to fear. His crook and staff protect and comfort you; the crook is His divine power, the staff His redeeming Cross. He has prepared a table for you, where He gives you spiritual food to fortify you against the assaults of evil spirits and temptations; and He has anointed your head with chrism, the oil of the Spirit. Finally He offers you the wine that gladdens your heart, the glorious chalice that Jesus Himself took into His hands at the Last Supper, saying: "This is My Blood which is shed for the forgiveness of sins."

You will find many other passages of Scripture that speak in this way of the sacraments. Take for instance that saying of Solomon, "Come, eat your bread with enjoyment, and drink your wine with a cheerful heart; let your head be anointed with oil, and your garments always be white, for the Lord has accepted what you have done" (Eccl. 9:7, 8). I am sure all of you will be able to give me a sacramental interpretation of this text, and of many another which you yourselves will be able to point out to me.

So we will end our lesson for today. Tomorrow we shall end our time together by returning to the subject of the spiritual combat and the armor the Lord has provided for you.

Chapter Twenty-three

Easter Saturday

The spiritual arena

My brothers and sisters, you have now entered fully into the mystery of Christ. You have received all the sacraments of initiation and know with the certainty of faith that you have been born again. Tomorrow you will be returning to your own homes and your ordinary employments. Before you go let me give you such teaching as I can on how to live your new life as children of God and athletes of Jesus Christ.

When you committed your lives to the Lord, you renounced Satan and all his worldly pomps. You must now show the sincerity of that renunciation and commitment by the way you live. Words and ceremonies are not enough. Your old enemy is extremely cunning; if he finds any backsliding in you after baptism, he will claim the right to drag you into slavery again.

So make sure your lives match your profession. The period preceding your initiation was a time of training, but from now on the arena is open to you and the contest has already begun. All eyes are upon you. The world is watching to see whether our Christian claim is true, and whether you really have found a new and mysterious source of strength. The angels too are watching to see what kind of fight you put up. Does not Saint Paul tell the Corinthians: "We have been made a spectacle to the whole world, both angels and men" (1 Cor. 4:9)? But have courage; the Lord of angels Himself presides over the contest, and He is by no means an impartial judge. How could He be? He gave His life for you, and it is all-important to Him that you should win.

In the Olympic Games the umpire takes his stand between the two rival parties without favoring either. He simply awaits the outcome. Not so in your struggle with the devil; the Lord is entirely on your side. When you entered the lists He Himself anointed you with spiritual power and shackled your adversary. If you stumble, He grasps you by the hand and sets you on your feet. As He promised in the Gospel, He has given you the power to tread underfoot snakes, scorpions, and all the forces of the enemy (Luke 10:19). Moreover, if the devil wins he is punished, whereas victory gains you a crown.

Be full of confidence then, and gird yourselves in readiness for the fray. The Lord has provided you with shining armor brighter than gold, stronger than any sword, keener than flame, lighter than the wind. Far from crushing you by its weight, it gives you wings. This is a new kind of armor, supplied by the Holy Spirit for a new kind of warfare—the spiritual combat. Men and women are pitted against demons; flesh and blood is obliged to defend itself against incorporeal powers. So it is no bronze shield, no iron breastplate that the Lord has fashioned for you, but the shield of faith and the breastplate of righteousness. In your hands you hold a sharp sword, the word of God that the Spirit gives you.

Take care not to return to your former servitude

I am speaking to all of you here; not just to the newly baptized, but to those of you who have been Christians for years. What I have to say applies to each one of us, because each of us has entered into a contract with Christ. We have acknowledged and accepted the sovereignty of the Lord God and renounced the service of the devil. Having made this commitment to the Lord, we must take care not to return to our former servitude all over again. Since Christ has canceled the bond that stood against us and destroyed it by nailing it to the Cross, let us make sure another is not drawn up.

Do not let yourselves slip back through carelessness. You have left Egypt; do not start looking round for a new state of bondage. Forget the clay and the bricks. The Israelites saw the Lord's mighty power at work when He led them out of Egypt, but you have experienced even greater wonders. Instead of seeing Pharaoh and his army drowning in the sea, you witnessed the devil and his forces swallowed up in the waters of baptism. The Israelites passed through the sea; you have passed through death to life. They were rescued from the Egyptians; you have been rescued from evil spirits. They were delivered from slavery in a foreign land; you have been delivered from something far worse—slavery to sin.

So from now on serve the Lord your God with joy and gratitude. He has taken away your sins and pardoned all your wrongdoing, and you can have complete confidence in His power to defend you against your adversary the devil and protect you from all the traps and snares with which he tries to make you sin against God. Commit yourselves wholly to Jesus Christ, and ask Him to be Lord of your life. Then you need have no fear of the devil.

You have put on Christ

Men who hold temporal office in the state wear a special badge which gains them public respect. They are careful to do nothing unworthy of their insignia; if ever they attempted to do so, there would be plenty of people to prevent them. Or if anyone bore them a grudge, their badge of office would protect them from insult or attack.

Now you do not merely wear a Christian badge; you have the blessed Trinity actually living in your soul. So you are under an even greater obligation to show yourselves worthy of respect, and to prove by your scrupulous conduct and watchfulness that you belong to the true King's service.

Soldiers too are immediately recognizable by their uniform; no words of explanation are required. So it is with us Christians. We have put on Christ; He has made His home in us. Without saying a word, we can witness to the power of His indwelling Spirit by the way we live.

During the past week your beautiful white garments have attracted everyone's attention. Even when you are no longer wearing them, you can still draw all who see you to glorify God and follow your example, by preserving the royal robe of your baptismal innocence in all its beauty, walking in the Spirit and serving the Lord with all your might. "Let your light shine before men," our Lord tells us in the Gospel, "in such a way that people will see your good works and be led to praise your heavenly Father" (Matt. 5:16). It is not by wearing a distinctive dress, but by their way of life that Christians attract unbelievers to the Lord. The light Jesus speaks of is the inner life of the spirit, radiating the beauty of the new life that is now yours and clarifying the minds of those who observe the change in you, so that their prejudices are dispelled and they are drawn to imitate you.

You must realize that the grace of enlightenment you received in baptism is not a gift for the initiated only. It is meant to be a beacon to others, showing them the way to reach the salvation you yourselves have discovered and enabling them to see the ugliness of their sins. The Lord wants your faith, your honesty, your humility, your loving service of your brothers and sisters to inspire all who see you to praise your heavenly Father for His transforming grace. So from now on do your utmost to live the kind of life that will make others want to share it.

As the blessed Apostle Paul tells us, all of you who have been baptized in Christ have clothed yourselves with Christ; you have put on Christ as a garment (Gal. 3:27). You have laid aside your old rags and received a garment of light. There is a radiance emanating from this robe that deflects the powers of darkness. Never let it be diminished. Rather, increase its brilliance by growing in holiness; in this way you will be doing your part to extend the Kingdom of God.

Jesus is the Way to the Father

My brothers and sisters, this is the last time I shall be speaking to you as a group. But you will always be my children in a very special way, because you are the fruit of my toil, my joy and my crown. You are the new offspring of Holy Mother Church, the proof of her fecundity, the gift of the Father. Yes, all of you who stand fast in the Lord and in the faith you have professed are as it were a holy seed, a swarm of bees about to leave the hive here and establish a new colony among your own people. So let my last exhortation to you all be in the words of Saint Paul: Put on the Lord Jesus Christ, and make no provision for the flesh and its desires; then you will be clothed with the risen life of Jesus, which you have received in these holy sacraments. All of you have been clothed with Christ by your baptism. There is no longer any difference between you, neither Jew nor Gentile, slave nor freeman, male nor female; you are all one in Christ Jesus (Rom. 13:12–14).

Such is the power of baptism. It is a sacrament of new life which begins here and now with the forgiveness of all your past sins, and will attain its fullness in the resurrection of the dead. While you are still in your mortal bodies you are walking by faith; but Jesus Christ, to whom your steps are directed, is

Himself the sure and certain way to the Father. "I am the Way," He told us. He has stored up overflowing happiness for all of us who believe in Him and honor His holy name, happiness that will be fully revealed and perfected when we arrive at the plenitude of reality which we already possess in hope.

At the end of Easter week, the newly baptized lay aside their white garments, and at last on the Second Sunday of Easter they take their place among the rest of the faithful in the congregation before returning to their own homes.

God our Father,
we give You thanks and praise
for the almighty power
with which You have freed Your people from death
and given them new and everlasting life
in the waters of baptism.
Today we celebrate the eighth day of their new birth.
Guard them always, body and soul,
so that they may know and understand
that it is to Your loving protection
that they owe the gift of perseverance
in the Holy Catholic Faith.
By the outpouring of Your grace
You continually increase the numbers of those who believe in
   You.
Look kindly, therefore, on the children of Your adoption,
and grant that all who have been reborn in these sacramental
   mysteries
may be found worthy of admittance
to Your heavenly Kingdom.
We make this prayer to You, almighty Father,
through Jesus Christ, Your only Son, our Lord,
who lives and reigns with You and Your Holy, life-giving
   Spirit,
one God,
for ever and ever.
Amen.[23]

VIII
EPILOGUE:
THE NEW LIFE IN
THE SPIRIT

A Personal Testimony
from Saint Cyprian to his friend Donatus

Carthage, A.D. 246

I promised to share with you the grace God in His great mercy has shown me, and to tell you as simply as I can what I have experienced since I was baptized.

Until that time I was still living in the dark, knowing nothing of my true life. I was completely involved in this world's affairs, influenced by all its changing moods and troubles, and exiled from the light of truth. I had indeed been told that God offered men and women a second birth by which we could be saved, but I very much doubted that I could change the kind of life I was then living. Frankly, I could not see how a person could cast off his fallen nature and be changed in heart and soul, while he still lived in the same body as before. How is it possible, I asked myself, to change the habits of a lifetime instantaneously? How can one suddenly rid oneself of accumulated guilt and break with sin that has become so deeply rooted in one's life? Can a man whose whole life-style is characterized by feasting and luxury learn frugality and simplicity in a single moment? A person who craves for public distinction and honors cannot bear to be passed over unnoticed; another who is accustomed to throngs of flattering attendants thinks it a terrible penance to be left alone. Is every species of temptation suddenly to lose its force? Shall we no longer feel the enticement of wine and good living? Will pride no longer swell our heads or anger blaze in our breasts? Shall we no longer be troubled by covetousness or cruelty or ambition or lust?

These were my thoughts. My past life was burdened with so many sins that I saw no way ever to be rid of, that I had grown accustomed to giving way to my weakness. I despaired of ever being any better. Consequently I simply humored my evil inclinations and made no attempt to combat them.

But at last I made up my mind to ask for baptism. I went down into those life-giving waters, and all the stains of my past were washed away. I committed my life to the Lord; He cleansed my heart and filled me with His Holy Spirit. I was born again, a new man.

Then, in a most marvelous way, all my doubts cleared up. I could now see what had been hidden from me before. I found I could do things that had previously been impossible. I saw that as long as I had been living according to my lower nature, I was at the mercy of sin and my course was set for death, but that by living according to my new birth in the Holy Spirit I had already begun to share God's eternal life.

You know as well as I do what sins I died to at that moment, just as you know the gifts the Holy Spirit gave me along with my new life. I have no desire to boast, but it is surely right to thank God for His free gift. It was through faith in Him that I received the power to break with the sins into which my own folly had led me.

All our power for good is God's gift; He is the source of our life and strength. Through Him we grow and mature, so as to experience even in this life a foretaste of what is to come. Only let us keep our hearts pure, and fear nothing so much as to lose our newly restored innocence; then the Lord, who has made the light of His grace shine in our hearts, will establish His home within us.

If we walk firmly and steadily in the Lord's ways, trusting in Him with all our heart and strength, all we have to do is to be what our baptism has made us. Freedom and power to do good will be given us in proportion to our spiritual growth. God does not measure His heavenly gift to us in the scales the way we mortals dispense earthly goods; He pours out His Spirit without stint, so that it flows freely on and on, never ceasing, continually abounding in endless generosity. We have only to open our hearts with longing and drink it in. The amount of grace we receive is measured by the faith with which we appropriate it. By that grace we are given power in all purity to heal the sick, whether of body or of mind, to reconcile enemies, to quell violence, to calm passions, to reprimand demons and force them to disclose their identity, punishing them with sharp blows until, with loud shrieks and struggles, they flee in terror. The blows we deal them are invisible, but what they effect is manifest to all. In so far as we are what we have begun to be, the Spirit is free to act through us, even though our bodily sight is still hindered by the cloud of this earth's dust.

How tremendous is this freedom and the spiritual power the Lord has given us! Not only are we protected from harm, but we are given authority over the whole force of the enemy who attacks us!

When I look back on the darkness from which I have escaped, I can only praise and thank God for the love He has shown me. My heart is filled with pity for all the people still trapped in that living death. Our civilization has surely reached the lowest depths of infamy; robbery, violence, murder on every side, the whole world reeking with blood; cruelty and bloodlust at the games, parricide and incest on the stage, perversion in private life, corruption in the administration of the law. Public office is purchased by flattery, wealth gained by dishonesty. Men are in bondage to money and luxury, yet they obstinately cling to the possessions from which neither they nor their families derive any profit. The more exalted a person's station, the greater is his fear of losing it. A ruler who denies peace to his subjects can find none for himself. What a price the world exacts for the honors and dignities it bestows!

True peace and security here below can only be attained by seeking deliverance from this turbulent world and accepting the salvation held out to us by God; in fixing our eyes on Jesus Christ, not on the earth. Then when we have been admitted to a share in the divine gift and have come to know the Lord, we discover that the things that seem so important to others are as nothing compared to the joy we now experience. We no longer seek the world's favors, because we have been raised above the world. How blessed it is to be released from earthly entanglements and to emerge from corruption into the light of eternity! All the mischief our old enemy has done us in the past is brought to nothing. When we see what we once were, it makes us love even more what we are to be.

We do not have to toil and sweat to achieve our own perfection, nor are money and influence needed to obtain the gift of the Holy Spirit. It is freely given by God, always available for us to use. Just as the sun shines and the day brings light, the stream irrigates the soil and rain waters the earth, so the heavenly Spirit pours itself into us. Once we have lifted our eyes to heaven and acknowledged our Creator, once we have been raised above the earth and rescued from slavery to this world, then we begin truly to be that new creation we believe ourselves to be.

We have received the seal of the Spirit. Our task now is to preserve the integrity of what we have received by living a truly Christian life. We must give time to prayer and the study of

Scripture, now speaking to God, now listening to His word to us and letting His teaching mold us. He has enriched us with a treasure no one can take away; we have eaten and drunk at His heavenly banquet, and can never again know the pinch of poverty. Magnificent palaces are as nothing in comparison with the glory of our own soul, which has become the Lord's temple with the Holy Spirit dwelling in it. As long as we keep it clean and open to the light, this temple of ours will never lose its beauty or fall into decay, until the day our bodies are restored to us from the grave and our whole being is brought to the perfect realization of God's plan for us.

Appendix I

The Liturgy of Holy Baptism and Chrismation in the Eastern Orthodox Church

For purposes of comparison, we include here a slightly abridged text of the liturgy of baptism and chrismation as practiced in the Eastern Church of the early centuries and the Orthodox Church today.

The Enrollment of Catechumens

The priest breathes three times in the form of a cross on the catechumen's face. Then he makes the sign of the cross on the catechumen's forehead three times, saying each time:

Priest: In the Name of the Father and of the Son and of the Holy Spirit, now and ever and unto ages of ages. Amen. *(three times)*

Deacon: Let us pray to the Lord.

People: Lord have mercy.

Priest lays his right hand on the head of the catechumen, saying:

Priest: In your Name, O Lord God of truth, and in the Name of your Only-begotten Son and of Your Holy Spirit, I lay my hand upon this *(these)* Your servant(s) *(name)* who have been accounted worthy to flee unto Your holy Name and to be sheltered under the shadow of Your wings. Remove far from him *(her/them)* that ancient error, and fill him *(her/them)* with faith and hope and love that is in You, that he *(she/they)* may know that You alone are the true God and Your Only-begotten Son, our Lord Jesus Christ, and Your Holy Spirit. Grant him *(her/them)* to walk in Your commandments and to observe those things that are acceptable before You, for if a man does these things he shall find life in them. Inscribe him *(her/them)* in Your Book of Life and unite him *(her/them)* to the flock of Your inheritance. Let Your holy Name be glorified in him *(her/them)* and that of Your well-beloved Son, our Lord Jesus Christ, and of your life-creating Spirit. Let Your eyes look upon him *(her/them)* in mercy, and Your ears be ever attentive unto the voice of his *(her/their)* prayer. Let him *(her/them)* ever rejoice in the works of his *(her/their)* hands, and in all his *(her/their)* generation, that he *(she/they)* may give thanks to You, worshipping and glorifying Your great and most high Name, ever praising You all the days of his *(her/their)* life. For all the powers of heaven praise You, and Yours is the glory, of the Father and of the Son and of the Holy Spirit, now and ever and unto ages of ages.

People: Amen.

The Prayers of Exorcism are prayed over all who are about to be baptized, whether they are adults or infants. There are four prayers in all, of which only the fourth is given here.
The catechumen is brought to the front of the church and faces west. The priest stands beside the catechumen, also facing west, but bowing east for the exclamation at the end of each prayer.

The Fourth Prayer of Exorcism

Deacon: Let us pray to the Lord.

People: Lord, have mercy.

Priest: O existing, sovereign Master and Lord, who made man after Your own image and likeness and gave to him power of eternal life; and when he had fallen through sin did not disdain him, but provided salvation for the world, through the incarnation of Your Christ. Redeem this *(these)* Your creature(s) from the yoke of the enemy, and receive him *(her/them)* into Your heavenly Kingdom. Open the eyes of his *(her/their)* understanding, so that the illumination of Your gospel may dawn upon him *(her/them)*. Yoke unto his *(her/their)* life a shining angel to deliver him *(her/them)* from every plot directed against him *(her/them)* by the adversary, from encounter with evil, from the noonday demon, and from evil visions.

The priest breathes three times on the catechumen's forehead, mouth, and breast, saying:

Drive out from him *(her/them)* every evil and unclean spirit, hiding and lurking in his *(her/their)* heart(s). *(three times)*
The spirit of error, the spirit of guile, the spirit of idolatry and of every lust, the spirit of deceit and of every uncleanness which operates through the prompting of the devil. Make him *(her/them)* (a) reason-endowed sheep of the holy flock of Your Christ, and (an) honorable member(s) of Your Church, (a) hallowed vessel(s), (a) child *(children)* of light, and (an) heir(s) of Your Kingdom, so that, having lived in accordance with Your commandment, and preserved the seal unbroken and kept his *(her/their)* garment(s) undefiled, he *(she/they)* may attain unto the blessedness of the saints of Your Kingdom. Through the grace and compassion and love for mankind of Your Only-begotten Son, with whom You are blessed, together with Your all-holy, good, and life-creating Spirit, now and ever and unto ages of ages.

People: Amen.

The Renunciation of Satan and the Profession of Faith

The priest asks the following questions and those to be baptized and/or chrismated answer together, or, in the case of infants, the parents and sponsors answer.

Priest: *(Asked three times.)* Do you renounce Satan and all his works, and all his worship, and all his angels, and all his service, and all his pride?

Catechumen: I do renounce him.

Priest: *(Asked three times.)* Have you renounced Satan?

Catechumen: I have renounced him.

Priest: Then blow and spit upon him.

When this is done, the priest says:

Priest: Turn to the east, and stand in reverence.

Then the priest asks three times and the catechumens respond three times:

Priest: Do you join Christ?

Catechumen: I do join Him.

Then the priest asks once:

Priest: Have you joined Christ?

Catechumen: I have joined Him.

Priest: And do you believe in Him?

Catechumen: I believe in Him as King and as God.

The catechumens say the Nicene Creed:

Catechumen: I believe in one God, the Father Almighty, Maker of heaven and earth, and of all things visible and invisible; and in one Lord Jesus Christ, the Son of God, the Only-begotten, Begotten of the Father before all worlds, Light of Light, Very God of Very God, Begotten, not made; of one essence with the Father, by whom all things were made: who for us men and for our salvation came down from heaven, was incarnate of the Holy Spirit and the Virgin Mary, and was made man; and was crucified also for us under Pontius Pilate, and suffered and was buried; and the third day He rose again, according to the Scriptures; and ascended into heaven, and sits at the right hand of the Father; and He shall come again with glory to judge the living and the dead; whose Kingdom shall have no end. And I believe in the Holy Spirit, the Lord and Giver of Life, who proceeds from the Father, who with the Father and the Son together is worshipped and glorified, who spoke by the prophets; and I believe in One Holy Catholic and Apostolic Church. I acknowledge one baptism for the remission of sins. I look for the resurrection of the dead, and the life of the world to come. Amen.

Then the priest asks three times and the catechumens respond three times:

Priest: Have you joined Christ?

Catechumen: I have joined Him.

Priest: Then bow down before Him and worship Him.

Each catechumen makes a low bow (or prostration), saying:

Catechumen: I worship Father, Son, and Holy Spirit, the Trinity, one in essence and undivided.

Priest: Blessed is God, who desires that all men should be saved and come to the knowledge of the truth, now and ever and unto ages of ages.

People: Amen.

Deacon: Let us pray to the Lord.

People: Lord, have mercy.

Priest: O sovereign Master, Lord our God, call these Your servants *(names)* to Your holy illumination, and account them worthy of this grace of Your holy baptism. Put off from them the old man, and renew them unto everlasting life; fill them with the power of Your Holy Spirit, unto union with Your Christ; that they may no longer be children of the body, but children of Your Kingdom. Through the good will and grace of Your Only-begotten Son, with whom You are blessed, together with Your all-holy, good, and life-creating Spirit, now and ever and unto ages of ages.

People: Amen.

The Blessing of the Baptismal Water

Deacon: Father, give the blessing.

Priest: Blessed is the Kingdom of the Father and of the Son and of the Holy Spirit, now and ever and unto ages of ages.

People: Amen.

The priest bows and prays:

Priest: O compassionate and merciful God, who try the minds and hearts, who alone know the secrets of men, for no deed is secret in Your sight, but all things are exposed and naked in Your sight, and who perceive that which concerns me: Do not turn away Your face from me, but overlook my offenses in this hour, O Lord, who overlook the sins of men which they repent. Wash away the defilement of my body and the stain of my soul. Completely sanctify me by Your all-powerful, invisible might, and by Your spiritual right hand, lest, by preaching liberty to others, and offering this in the perfect faith of Your unspeakable love for mankind, I may be condemned as a servant of sin. O sovereign Master, who alone are good and loving, let me not be turned away humbled and shamed, but send forth to me power from on high, and strengthen me for the administration of this Your present, great and most heavenly mystery. Form the image of Your Christ in them who are about to be born again through my humility. Build them on the foundation of Your apostles and prophets. Do not cast them down, but plant them as a plant of truth in Your Holy, Catholic, and Apostolic Church, and do not pluck them out. That, by their advancing in piety, by them may be glorified Your most holy Name, of Father and of Son and of Holy Spirit, now and ever and unto ages of ages.

People: Amen.

The Great Prayer for the Blessing of the Water

Priest: Great are You, O Lord, and wondrous are Your works, and no word will suffice to sing of Your wonders! *(three times)*
For by Your will You have brought all things from nothingness into being and by Your power sustain all creation, and by Your providence direct the world. You from the four elements have formed creation and have crowned the cycle of the year with the

four seasons; all the spiritual powers tremble before You; the sun praises You; the moon glorifies You; the stars in their courses meet with You; the light hearkens unto You; the depths shudder at Your presence; the springs of water serve You; You have stretched out the heavens as a curtain; You have founded the earth upon the waters; You bounded the sea with sand; You have poured forth the air for breathing; the angelic powers minister unto You; the choirs of archangels worship before You; the many-eyed cherubim and the six-winged seraphim, as they stand and fly around You, veil themselves with fear of Your unapproachable glory.

For You, being boundless and without beginning and unutterable, came down on earth, taking the form of a servant, being made in the likeness of men; for You, O Master, through the tenderness of Your mercy, could not endure the race of men tormented by the devil, but You came and saved us. We confess Your grace; we proclaim Your beneficence; we do not hide Your mercy. You have set at liberty the generations of our nature; You hallowed the virgin's womb by Your birth; all creation praises You, who revealed Yourself, for You were seen upon the earth, and sojourned with men. You hallowed the streams of Jordan, sending down from the heavens Your Holy Spirit, and crushed the heads of dragons that lurked therein.

Do You Yourself, O loving King, be present now also through the descent of Your Holy Spirit and hallow this water. Do You Yourself, O loving King, be present now also through the descent of Your Holy Spirit and hallow this water. Do You Yourself, O loving King, be present now also through the descent of Your Holy Spirit and hallow this water. Give to it the grace of redemption, the blessing of Jordan. Make it a fountain of incorruption, a gift of sanctification, a loosing of sins, a healing of sicknesses, a destruction of demons, unapproachable by hostile powers, filled with angelic might; and let them that take counsel together against Your creature flee therefrom, for I have called upon Your Name, O Lord, which is wonderful, and glorious, and terrible unto adversaries.

The priest dips his fingers in the water and makes the sign of the cross three times on the water, breathing on it and saying each time:

Let all adverse powers be crushed beneath the signing of Your most precious cross. *(three times)*

We pray You, O Lord, let every airy and invisible specter withdraw itself from us, and let not a demon of darkness conceal himself in this water; neither let an evil spirit, bringing obscurity of purpose and rebellious thoughts, descend into it with those who are about to be baptized.

But, O Master of all, declare this water to be water of redemption, water of sanctification, a cleansing of flesh and spirit, a gift of sonship, a garment of incorruption, a fountain of life. For You have said, O Lord, "Wash, and be clean; put away evil from Your souls." You have bestowed upon us regeneration from on high by water and the Spirit.

Manifest Yourself, O Lord, in this water, and grant that those who are to be baptized may be transformed therein to the putting away of the old man, which is corrupt according to the deceitful lusts, and to the putting on of the new, which is renewed according to the image of Him that created them. That being planted in the likeness of Your death through baptism, they may attain unto the prize of their high calling, and be accounted among the number of the firstborn, whose names are written in heaven, in You our God and Lord, Jesus Christ, to whom be all glory and might, together with Your eternal Father and with Your all-holy, good, and life-creating Spirit, now and ever and unto ages of ages.

People: Amen.

The Anointing with the Oil

The deacon brings a vessel of olive oil to the priest. The priest breathes three times on the vessel and makes the sign of the cross over it three times.

Deacon: Let us pray to the Lord.

People: Lord, have mercy.

Priest: Sovereign Lord and Master, God of our Fathers, who sent to those in the ark of Noah a dove bearing a twig of olive in its beak as a sign of reconciliation and salvation from the flood, and through these things prefigured the mystery of grace; and thereby have filled them that were under the law with the Holy Spirit, and perfected them that are under grace: Bless this oil by the power and operation and descent of the Holy Spirit that it may become an anointing of incorruption, a shield of righteousness, a renewal of soul and body, an averting of every operation of the devil, to the removal of all evils from them that are anointed with it in faith, to Your glory, and to that of Your Only-begotten Son and of Your all-holy, good, and life-creating Spirit, now and ever and unto ages of ages.

People: Amen.

The priest takes the vessel of oil and pours a little oil on the water three times in the form of a cross. Meanwhile the people/choir sing:

Alleluia *(three times).*

When this is done the priest exclaims:

Priest: Blessed is God who enlightens and sanctifies every man that comes into the world, now and ever and unto ages of ages.

People: Amen.

The priest (with assistants, if there are many to be baptized) anoints each catechumen with the sign of the cross, saying:

Priest: *(on the forehead)* The servant of God *(name)* is anointed with the oil of gladness in the name of the Father and of the Son and of the Holy Spirit.
(on the breast and back) . . . for the healing of soul and body.
(on the ears) . . . for the hearing of the faith.
(on the hands) . . .Your hands, O Lord, have made me and fashioned me.
(on the feet) . . . that he/she may walk in the paths of Your commandments.

The Baptism

The priest, facing east, immerses each catechumen (or infant) three times, saying:

Priest: The servant of God *(name)* is baptized in the Name of the Father . . .

People: Amen.

Priest: and of the Son . . .

People: Amen.

Priest: and of the Holy Spirit . . .

People: Amen.

After each person is baptized, the priest immediately gives him a white robe, saying:

Priest: The servant of God *(name)* is clothed with the garment of righteousness in the Name of the Father and of the Son and of the Holy Spirit.

When all have been baptized, the people/choir sing the following refrain with verses from Psalm 31/32 sung in between.

People: Grant unto me the robe of Light, for You clothe Yourself with Light, O Most Merciful Christ our God.

The Sacrament of Holy Chrismation

When the newly baptized have been clothed in their white garments and have reassembled, we continue.

Deacon: Let us pray to the Lord.

People: Lord, have mercy.

Priest: Blessed are You, Lord God Almighty, Fountain of blessings, Sun of righteousness, who have made to shine forth for those in darkness the light of salvation through the manifestation of Your Only-begotten Son and our God, granting unto us, though we are unworthy, blessed cleansing in holy water, and divine sanctification in the life-effecting anointing; who now also have been well-pleased to regenerate these Your servants newly illuminated through water and the Spirit, giving them forgiveness of their voluntary and involuntary sins: Do You Yourself, sovereign Master, compassionate King of all, bestow upon them also the seal of Your almighty Holy Spirit, and the communion of the holy Body and most precious Blood of Your Christ; keep them in Your sanctification; confirm them in the Orthodox Faith; deliver them from the evil one and all his devices; preserve their souls, through Your saving fear, in purity and righteousness, that in every work and word, being acceptable before You, they may become children and heirs of Your heavenly Kingdom. For You are our God, the God of mercy and salvation, and to You we give glory, to the Father and to the Son and to the Holy Spirit, now and ever and unto ages of ages.

People: Amen.

The Anointing with Holy Chrism

The priest then anoints each person with the holy chrism on the forehead, the eyes, the nostrils, the lips, the ears, the breast, the hands, and the feet, saying each time:

Priest: The seal of the gift of the Holy Spirit.

People: Seal!

The Baptismal Procession

When all have been chrismated, the deacon with the censer and the priest with the cross lead the newly baptized in a procession around or into the church. During this procession the people sing:

People: As many as have been baptized into Christ have put on Christ. Alleluia. *(three times)*
Glory to the Father and to the Son and to the Holy Spirit, now and ever and unto ages of ages. Amen.

Washing Off the Chrism / The Ablution

Deacon: Let us pray to the Lord.

People: Lord, have mercy.

Priest: O sovereign Master and Lord, who through holy baptism have granted forgiveness of sins to these Your servants, bestowing on them a life of regeneration: let the light of Your countenance evermore shine in their hearts, maintain the shield of their faith against the plotting of enemies; preserve in them the garment of incorruption, which they have put on undefiled and unstained; preserve in them the seal of Your grace, being gracious unto us, and unto them according to the multitude of Your mercies. Lay upon them Your mighty hand, and guard them in the power of Your goodness. Preserve unspotted their pledge of faith in You. Account them worthy of life everlasting and Your good favor.
For You are our sanctification, and to You we give glory: to the Father and to the Son and to the Holy Spirit, now and ever and unto ages of ages.

People: Amen.

Priest: Peace be to all.

People: And to your spirit.

Deacon: Bow your heads to the Lord.

People: To You, O Lord.

Priest: Those who have put on You, O Christ, with us bow their heads unto You; ever protect them as warriors invincible against those who vainly raise up enmity against them, or, as might be, against us; and by Your crown of incorruption declare us all to be victorious in the end.
For Yours it is to have mercy and to save, and to You we give glory, together with Your eternal Father and Your all-holy, good, and life-creating Spirit, now and ever and unto ages of ages.

People: Amen.

The priest takes the sponge and washes off the chrism, saying to each newly baptized person:

Priest: You are justified. You are illumined. You are anointed with the holy chrism. You are sanctified. You are washed clean, in the Name of the Father and of the Son and of the Holy Spirit.

People: Amen.

On the eighth day after baptism, the newly illumined come for tonsure.

The Tonsure

Deacon: Let us pray to the Lord.

People: Lord, have mercy.

Priest: O Master, Lord our God, who have honored man with Your own image and have fashioned him from a soul endowed with reason and a beautiful body to serve the soul, You have set on high the head and have wonderfully endowed it with the highest senses, and have covered it with hair, that it might be protected from the changes of weather; You have fitly joined together all his members, that with them all men may give thanks to You, the supreme Creator.
And through Your chosen vessel, the Apostle Paul, You also have given us a commandment that we should do all things to Your glory: Bless, now, Your servants, *(names)*, who are here to make a first offering cut from the hair of their heads, and grant that they may exercise themselves in Your law, and do those things which are well pleasing in Your sight. For You are a merciful God and love mankind, and to You we give glory, to the Father and to the Son and to the Holy Spirit, now and ever and unto ages of ages.

People: Amen.

Priest: Peace be to all.

People: And to your spirit.

Deacon: Bow your heads to the Lord.

People: To You, O Lord.

Priest: O Lord our God, who by Your goodness sanctify, through the fulfilling of the baptismal font, those who believe in You: Bless these Your servants and let Your blessing descend on their heads. And as You blessed King David by the hand of Your Prophet Samuel, bless also the head of Your servants (*names*) by the hand of me, a sinner, inspiring them with Your Holy Spirit; that as they increase in stature, and even unto a ripe old age, they may send up glory to You, and behold the good things of Jerusalem all the days of their life. For to You are due all glory, honor, and worship, to the Father and to the Son and to the Holy Spirit, now and ever and unto ages of ages.

People: Amen.

The priest takes scissors and cuts four snips of hair from the four sides of the head, saying to each newly baptized person:

Priest: The servant of God is tonsured in the Name of the Father and of the Son and of the Holy Spirit.

People: Amen.

The priest pinches the cut hairs in the scissors and burns them in a candle.

Appendix II

Those who were kind enough to read this book in typescript have asked two questions that should perhaps be answered here. The first is, "How much of this is the Fathers speaking, and how much is just you?" The other is, "What validity is there in the patristic teaching on the senses of Scripture?"

Perhaps the best way to answer the first question is to explain how the book has been compiled. The first task was to assemble and study all the available texts, together with any relevant liturgical documents and commentaries, in order to become thoroughly familiar with the ancient catechetical tradition and the ceremonies connected with the rites of initiation as they were carried out in different parts of the world in the fourth and early fifth centuries. Fortunately an English translation of Ambrose and Cyril was available; the remaining texts had to be put into a rough literal translation for working purposes. Next this material was sorted out and collated under various headings, so that the order to be followed and which of the sources to use at different stages of the rites could be decided.

In some sections there was a superabundance of texts to choose from; consequently many beautiful passages had to be left aside. Where there were a number of parallel texts I aimed at constructing a synthesis of the ideas contained in them, selecting strands from each and weaving them together.

A paragraph on pages 155–56, in the section *Crossing the Red Sea,* may serve as an example. The passage reads:

> The Israelites are oppressed by the Egyptians, so God sends Moses into Egypt to lead them out of the bondage to Pharaoh. The human race is enslaved to sin, so God sends Jesus Christ into the world to be their Savior and rescue them from bondage to Satan. The blood of the Passover lamb on their doorposts protects the Israelites from the Destroyer; the blood of the unblemished Lamb on the Cross puts demons to flight. Pharaoh pursues the people of Israel as far as the Red Sea; Satan pursues the people of God to the very waters of salvation. Moses divides the sea for the Israelites to pass through; Jesus opens the gates of death and shatters its iron bars. The tyrant of old is drowned in the sea; our tyrant is drowned in the waters of baptism, and our enmity with God destroyed. The people come forth from the sea whole and unscathed; we come up from the font as living from the dead, saved by the grace of Him who called us.

In comparison, here are the passages from various patristic sources that provided the material for this paragraph:

> Cyril, *Myst. Lect.* I, 2–3: "There we have Moses sent from God into Egypt; here, Christ sent by His Father into the world; there, that Moses might lead forth an oppressed people out of Egypt; here, that Christ might rescue mankind who are whelmed under sins; there, the blood of a lamb was the spell against the destroyer; here, the blood of the unblemished lamb Jesus Christ is made the charm to scare evil spirits; there, the tyrant pursued even to the sea that ancient people; and in like manner this daring and shameless spirit, the author of evil, followed thee, even to the very streams of

salvation. The tyrant of old was drowned in the sea; and this present one disappears in the salutary water." (English translation by R.W. Church in the *Library of the Fathers*)

Aphrahat, *Demonstration* XII, 8: "Moses diverted the sea for them and made them pass through it; our savior opens hell and shatters its portals, when He went down into it and opened and marked out the way for all who were to believe in Him."

Basil, *On the Holy Spirit* XIV: "The sea is the type of baptism, for it preserved them from Pharaoh as does this font from the tyranny of the devil. In the sea the enemy was slain, and in the baptismal waters our enmity with God is destroyed. The people came out of the sea whole and unscathed, while we come up from the font as living from the dead, saved by the grace of the one who called us."

In the preface I explained that the texts have been translated very freely, edited, paraphrased, abridged, or amplified in whatever way seemed to serve the purpose best. If the *Crossing of the Red Sea* is an example of editing, perhaps an example of paraphrasing may be taken from Saint Cyprian's Treatise on the Grace of God which is used in the Epilogue. This treatise was addressed to Cyprian's close friend Donatus shortly after his baptism in A.D. 246, and reflects the ornate rhetorical style taught in the schools of his day. Saint Augustine remarks that Cyprian's style was later "pruned of its redundance by the soundness of Christian doctrine, and subdued into a more grave and sober eloquence" *(On Christian Doctrine* IV, 24). Here is an exact translation of the beginning of the Epilogue, made by the Rev. Charles Thornton for the Oxford *Library of the Fathers:*

For me, while I yet lay in darkness and bewildering night, and was tossed to and fro on the billows of this troublesome world, ignorant of my true life, an outcast from light and truth, I used to think that second birth, which Divine Mercy promised for my salvation, a hard saying according to the life I then led: as if a man could be so quickened to a new life in the Laver of healing water, as to put off his natural self; and keep his former tabernacle, yet be changed in heart and soul!

In paraphrase, this passage becomes:

Until that time I was still living in the dark, knowing nothing of my true life. I was completely involved in this world's affairs, influenced by all its changing moods and troubles, and exiled from the light of truth. I had indeed been told that God offered men and women a second birth by which we could be saved, but I very much doubted that I could change the kind of life I was living. Frankly, I could not see how a person could cast off his fallen nature and be changed in heart and soul, while he still lived in the same body as before.

The need for abridgement can be seen most clearly in the writing of Theodore of Mopsuestia, whose teaching method was evidently based on the time-honored principle of dinning the lesson into his class through constant repetition. The following is a literal translation of part of his fourteenth catechetical homily:

In baptism the sign of this new birth is accomplished, that true second birth which will be manifested in its reality and given you when you rise from the dead and recover what death has taken from you. Clearly when a person is born he comes into existence, while he who dies goes out of existence. You will obtain new birth, then, by rising from the dead, and by this means a new existence will be granted to you, just as, when you were born of a woman, you came into existence, that existence of which death has deprived you. You will have this in actuality at the time predestined for you to be born again through the resurrection; for the time being you put your faith in Christ our Lord. Because these blessings are still in the future, it is necessary to receive them in symbols and signs by means of this awe-inspiring sacrament.

As abridged for use in the section *Water and the Spirit* on page 122, the above reads:

At the general resurrection of the dead on the Last Day, this new birth will be visibly manifested. In the meantime, through faith in Jesus Christ, we receive new life by means of signs and symbols.

Saint Ambrose's discourses, on the other hand, give the impression of having been hastily taken down as notes while he spoke. They generally need some amplification to make his meaning easier to follow. For example, the following passage from his Treatise on the Sacraments III, 2 was expanded in the section on *The healing of the man born blind,* page 167. In the original, it reads:

Another Evangelist told of the cure of a blind man; Matthew did, Luke did, Mark did. What does John alone say? "He took clay, and anointed his eyes, and said unto him, Go to Siloam. And rising, he went, and washed, and came seeing."

With amplification, this becomes:

Matthew, Mark, and Luke all describe the cure of blind men, but only John reports that Jesus spat on the ground and made clay which He applied to the eyes of a man who had been blind from birth, telling him to go and wash it off in the pool called Siloam. Then he tells us that the blind man went off and bathed his eyes; when he came back he was able to see.

In a few places, practical instructions have been inserted on the basis of allusions found in other patristic writings or liturgical documents. For example, on page 133 the candidates are told to wash themselves in readiness for their new birth.

This is based on a sentence in one of Saint Augustine's letters, in which he gives the following reason for the custom of taking a bath on Maundy Thursday:

> *Epist.* 54:7, 10 PL 33:204: ". . . because the bodies of the candidates had become dirty by the Lenten observance and could not be handled at the font without giving offense to the senses;"

and also on a rubric given in the Apostolic Tradition, a liturgical document dating from the third century:

> *Ap. Trad.* 20:5: "Let those who are to be baptized be instructed to wash and cleanse themselves on the fifth day of the week."

Fourth-century sources have also been used wherever possible for the prayers given at the end of each division of the book, though again these are treated freely. Sometimes the only available text was that given in the Gelasian Sacramentary, which is dated about the middle of the eighth century, though it contains a good deal of older material. The text of the exorcisms comes from this collection, but the form may well have been less fixed in earlier centuries.

To the question, then, "How much of this is the Fathers speaking and how much is just you?" I would answer that very little of it is "just me." Even though it is not a straightforward translation of patristic texts, I hope the Fathers would acknowledge that this series of lectures contains a faithful presentation of their own teaching; and also that they would pardon the liberties I have taken with their expression of it.

The second question, "How valid is the patristic teaching on the senses of Scripture?" is not easy to answer without embarking on a lengthy essay. However, in Chapter 18 Saint Ambrose lays down the principle that all Scripture has a literal, a moral, and a spiritual sense. I imagine no one would quarrel seriously with that statement. Biblical scholars stress the primary need to understand the literal meaning of any text, while Christians have always looked for moral guidance in God's word, following Saint Paul's admonition that what happened to the Israelites in the Old Testament was written down as a warning to us. It is in the interpretation of the spiritual sense of Scripture that we do not always agree.

That the events of the Old Testament were figures or types whose fullness is realized in Christ and the Church is one of the principles of biblical theology. What was prefigured historically is fulfilled spiritually. This is what the Fathers mean by the spiritual sense. We can say that typology is a genuine sense of Scripture contained in the text itself; instead of limiting the meaning of the text to past history, it takes it into the divine continuity of the revealed word, which is open to the future and the fulfillment of God's promises.

The Fathers had a profound understanding of this principle. Their overall grasp of the spiritual significance of the Bible is beyond doubt. In their interpretation of individual verses, however, they sometimes disconcert us by discovering apparent correspondences which have no connection with the literal sense of the text. Here they enter the field of allegory, an artificial method very popular in the early Church, especially in Alexandrian circles, where it originated with Philo, the Jewish exegete.

Chapter 20 contains part of Saint Ambrose's interpretation of the Song of Songs which, in common with the other Church Fathers, he understands as the expression of Christ's love for the Church and for each baptized Christian. This is a legitimate development of the literal sense of the text. But the application of individual verses of the Song of Songs to different aspects of Christian initiation is perhaps of unequal value. Sometimes it is based on other scriptural passages; at other times it is founded on allegorical analogies. Even these latter, however, should be given respect, since they appear to be drawn from an ancient common tradition. Many of the Fathers interpret the verse, "I have put off my garment; am I to put it on again?" (Song 5:3) in a baptismal sense, and the comparison of the Bride's teeth with a flock of sheep coming up from the washing (4:2) is widely used as a description of the newly baptized. Saint Augustine's comment on this imagery shows the delight the ancients took in such interpretations. In his treatise *On Christian Doctrine* he says:

> Someone could say that the lives of holy men are used to attract pagans to the Christian faith. These servants of God have laid down the burden of their sins in the baptismal font, and subsequently, through the gift of the Holy Spirit, yield a twofold fruit, namely the love of God and love of neighbor. But this plain statement would not please his audience nearly so much as the elucidation of the same meaning from that passage in the Song of Songs where the Church is praised under the figure of a beautiful woman: "Your teeth are like a flock of sheep newly shorn and coming up from the washing, each of them bearing twins, and none barren among them." Does the hearer learn any more than when he listens to the

same thought expressed in plain language, without the help of imagery? And yet, somehow, it gives me greater pleasure to think of the saints as the teeth of the Church, fastening into pagans and tearing them away from their errors, and bringing them into the Church's body with all their harsh edges softened as if they had been chewed by teeth! I love to recognize them under the figure of sheep newly shorn, laying down their sinful burdens like fleeces, coming up from the baptismal washing and all bearing twins, that is fulfilling the twofold commandment of love, none of them barren of the fruit of holiness.

Perhaps it is less true today that this kind of imagery gives people greater pleasure than the plain statement. Tastes change. For this reason I have allowed the need to keep the postbaptismal lectures within bounds to curtail the more allegorical passages; omitting, for example, Saint Ambrose's comparison of the newly baptized with budding fruit trees, and his interpretation of the Holy of Holies, where the Jewish high priest entered once a year, as the baptistery which the bishop enters annually during the Easter vigil.

However, all the explanations of the great Old Testament types of the Christian sacraments found in the common catechetical tradition are included in Chapters 18 to 21 (though one wonders why the story of the miraculous food given to Elijah by an angel in the desert to fortify him on his journey [1 Kings 19] is not numbered among the types of the Eucharist). All these interpretations belong to the genuine typological sense of Scripture.

Many difficulties with patristic interpretations of Scripture disappear when we realize that the Fathers did not set out to teach biblical exegesis, but Christian doctrine. All their thought and turn of speech was biblical; their sermons are often a tissue of scriptural allusions, and it was natural for them to use scriptural illustrations of everything they taught. Even when they employed allegorical methods, these served as a springboard for their presentation of doctrinal truths. They saw such procedures as justified by Saint Paul's statement that all Scripture is inspired by God and is useful for teaching (2 Tim. 3:16). So when we read the Fathers we should not allow ourselves to be put off by their questionable explanations of certain texts, but look for the underlying teaching of the Christian Faith.

Bibliography

Ambrose
On the Mysteries and *Treatise on the Sacraments.* Translated by T. Thompson. Edited by J. H. Strawley. London: SPCK, 1919. (DM, DS)
Des Sacrements, Des Mysteres, l'Explication du Symbole. Edited by B. Botte. Sources Chretiennes, 25 bis. Paris: Editions du Cerf, 1961.
Augustine
Sermons. Edited by J. P. Migne. Patrologia Latina, 38, 39, 40, 46. (S)
Sermons pour la Pacque. Edited by S. Poque. Sources Chretiennes, 116. Paris: Editions du Cerf, 1966.
First Catechetical Instruction. Translated by J. P. Christopher. Ancient Christian Writers, 2. Westminster, Maryland: Newman Press, 1946.
Chromatius
Sermons. Edited by J. Lemaire. Sources Chretiennes, 154. Paris: Editions du Cerf, 1969.
John Chrysostom
Huit Catecheses Baptismales. Edited by A. Wenger. Sources Chretiennes, 50 bis. Paris: Editions du Cerf, 1970. (BC)
Cyprian
Treatises. Translated by C. Thornton. Library of the Fathers. Oxford: J. H. Parker, 1899.
Cyril of Jerusalem
The Catechetical Lectures. Edited by W. Telfer. Library of Christian Classics, 4. London: SCM Press, 1965. (CL)
St. Cyril of Jerusalem's Lectures on the Christian Sacraments. Edited by F. L. Cross. London: SPCK, 1951. (ML)

Quodvultdeus
Sermons on the Creed. Edited by J. P. Migne. Patrologia Latina, 40, 41.
Sarapion
Bishop Sarapion's Prayer Book. Edited by J. Wordsworth. London: SPCK, 1915.
Theodore of Mopsuestia
Homelies Catechetiques. Edited by R. Tonneau and R. Devreesse. Rome: Vatican Press, 1949. (CH)
Tertullian
Treatise on Baptism. Translated by C. Dodgson. Library of the Fathers. Oxford: J. H. Parker, 1842.
Other Sources
Early Christian Prayers. Translated by W. Mitchell. Edited by A. Hamman. London: Longmans, Green, & Co., and Chicago: Henry Regnery, 1961.
Egeria's Travels. Edited by J. Wilkinson. London: SPCK, 1971.
The Gelasian Sacramentary. Edited by H. A. Wilson. Oxford: Clarendon Press, 1894.
Prayers from Eastern Liturgies. Edited by D. Attwater. London: Burns, Oates, & Washbourne, Ltd., 1931.
The Sacramentary. Edited by I. Schuster. London: Burns, Oates, & Washbourne, Ltd., 1924.
General Works on Patristic Catechesis
Danielou, Jean. *The Bible and the Liturgy.* Notre Dame: University of Notre Dame Press, 1961.
Danielou, Jean. *From Shadows to Reality.* London: Burns & Oates, 1960.
Dictionnaire d'Archeologie et de Liturgie. Edited by F. Cabrol and H. Leclercq. Paris: Letouzey et Ane, 1907–1950. Articles on baptism, exorcism, and the creed. (DACL)
Dudden, F. Homes. *The Life and Times of St. Ambrose.* Oxford: Clarendon Press, 1935.
Jungman, J. A. *The Early Liturgy.* Notre Dame: University of Notre Dame Press, 1959.
De Latte, Robert. "Saint Augustin et le Bapteme: Etude Liturgico-historique du rituel baptismal des adultes chez St. Augustin." *Questions Liturgiques,* no. 4, pp. 177–224. Mont-Cesar, 1975.
Lecuyer, Joseph. "Theologie de l'Initiation chretienne chez les Peres." *Maison-Dieu* 58, 1959, pp. 5–26.
Yarnold, Edward. *The Awe-Inspiring Rites of Initiation.* London: St. Paul Publications, 1971.

Index to Sources

Summary of Sources by Chapter

Chapter 1: Cyril, CL *Protocatechesis*.

Chapter 2: Chrysostom, BC I; Augustine, S 216; Cyril, CL I.

Chapter 3: Cyril, CL II; Augustine, S 216 (one sentence only).

Chapter 4: Chrysostom, BC II; Theodore, CH XII; Ambrose, DS II; Augustine, S 216.

Chapter 5: Theodore, CH I.

Chapter 6: Chrysostom, BC II; Cyril, CL V; Theodore, CH I; Augustine, *On the Creed for the Catechumens*.

Chapter 7: Augustine, S 212, 213, 214, *On the Creed for the Catechumens;* Cyril, CL XVI; Ignatius of Antioch, *Letter to the Romans* VII:3 (one sentence only).

Chapter 8: Augustine, S 212, 213, 214; Ambrose, *Explanation of the Creed*.

Chapter 9: Augustine, S. Guelferbytanus I; *On the Creed for the Catechumens* 11; S 58, 216; Chrysostom, BC II.

Solemn Exorcisms: *The Gelasian Sacramentary* I, xxxiii. Rubrics derived from *The Sacramentary*, v. 2, pp. 123–125, and from the article "Symbole" in DACL 1768.

Chapter 10: Augustine, S 56–59, 215; Theodore, CH XI.

Chapter 11: Augustine, S 56–59.

Chapter 12: Augustine, S 57; Theodore, CH XI; Ambrose, DS V.

Chapter 13: Theodore, CH XII.

Chapter 14: Theodore, CH XII, XIII; Cyril, ML I; Chrysostom, BC II.

Chapter 15: Cyril, CL III; Theodore, CH XIV; Cyril, ML II; Ambrose, DS I, III; Chrysostom, BC II.

Chapter 16: Ambrose, DS II, III, IV; Cyril, CL III, XVIII; ML II, III; Theodore, CH XIV; Chrysostom, BC I, II; Quodvultdeus, *Sermons on the Creed.*

Chapter 17: Ambrose, DM, DS I, IV; *Commentary on Psalm 36* i; Augustine, S 227, 229; Tertullian, *Treatise on Baptism;* Zeno, *Sermons on Exodus;* Didymus, *On the Trinity* XIV; Aphrahat, *Demonstration* XII; Basil, *On the Holy Spirit* XIV. See appendix on this section.

Chapter 18: Ambrose, DM, DS I–IV; *Commentary on Luke* x; *On the Holy Spirit* I, 6.

Chapter 19: Ambrose, DM, DS I–III; Chromatius, *Sermons* 14.

Chapter 20: Ambrose, DM, DS III–VI; Cyril, ML III–IV.

Chapter 21: Augustine, S 3; Ambrose, DM, DS IV–VI; Cyril, ML IV; Theodore, CH XVI.

Chapter 22: Ambrose, DM, DS V–VI; Chrysostom, *On 1 Corinthians;* Cyril, ML IV.

Chapter 23: Ambrose, DM, DS V–VI; Quodvultdeus, *Sermons on the Creed* III; Chrysostom, BC III–IV; Augustine, *Sermons for the Octave Day of Easter* VIII.

Epilogue: Cyprian, *Treatise to Donatus on the Grace of God.*

Index by Source Author

Notes

1. *Egeria's Travels,* 46:2–3.
2. Ambrose, DM I, i.
3. *Egeria's Travels,* 46:6.
4. *The Gelasian Sacramentary* I, xxx.
5. The whole of the sermon on which the last two paragraphs are based is a tissue of scriptural allusions.
6. *Bishop Sarapion's Prayer Book,* 21.
7. This was the version of the Apostles' Creed used in the West in the time of Augustine and Ambrose. It will be noticed that two clauses contained in our present version are omitted. "He descended into hell" was in fact not incorporated into the Apostles' Creed until the sixth century. "The communion of saints" is also a later addition; it was understood as an explanatory phrase describing "the Holy Catholic Church."
8. Prayer of the church of Antioch, fourth century. See A. Wenger, *Jean Chrysostome: Huit Catecheses Baptismales,* pp. 70–71.
9. Based on prayers from the Armenian and Byzantine rites. See *Prayers from the Eastern Liturgies,* ed. Attwater, pp. 68–72.
10. See *The Gelasian Sacramentary* I, xxxvi.
11. This teaching does not preclude the existence or malicious activity of spiritual angels of Satan (i.e. demons).
12. In Theodore's text at this point all these false teachers are named and their various errors enumerated.
13. Concerned as they were with the tendency of their contemporaries to defer the reception of baptism, the Fathers insisted emphatically on its necessity. Later Church teaching clarified that while baptism is

normative, God in His grace can and does save people outside the sacraments of the Church if, through no fault of their own, they are unable to be baptized.

14. *The Gelasian Sacramentary* I, xli.

15. Rite of the church of Constantinople, attributed to St. Proclus. See Wenger, *op. cit.,* p. 85; also the article "Symbole" in DACL 1768.

16. Some liturgical scholars hold that the candidate was required not merely to breathe but to *spit* in the devil's face, and this practice is observed in some eastern rites at the present day. My personal opinion, for what it is worth, is that the gesture in question was a cross between the two, i.e., what nowadays is commonly called a "raspberry"!

17. *Bishop Sarapion's Prayer Book,* 9.

18. Constantinople rite, see Wenger, *op. cit.,* p. 90.

19. *Bishop Sarapion's Prayer Book,* 15.

20. Roman Missal for Monday of Easter week.

21. In Milan there was a second anointing given by a priest as the neophyte came up from the font, distinct from the sacrament of chrismation which the bishop later administered. St. Ambrose attaches his teaching on the royal priesthood of the faithful to this second, rather indeterminate, anointing.

Elsewhere, however, the teaching on the royal priesthood was connected with chrismation. An extra anointing was given before baptism in some places. I have simplified the rite at this point, I hope without loss to the doctrine taught.

22. Literally, *quod est figura corporis et sanguinis Domini nostri Jesu Christi.* Figure, sign, symbol, likeness, representation, etc., are the only words we have in English to translate the sacramental terminology of the early Church. They must be understood in the sense so carefully explained by the Fathers, i.e., that the figure, etc., contains the reality it symbolizes. Clearly, St. Ambrose is not saying that the bread and wine are merely symbols of Christ's Body and Blood, since he expressly teaches that the Body and Blood are really present. The eucharistic prayer he quotes is very close to the Roman Canon.

23. *The Gelasian Sacramentary* I, liii.

Biographical Notes

Saint Ambrose: born in Trier about A.D. 339. Appointed governor of the Roman Province of Aemilia-Liguria, residing in Milan. Though only a catechumen at the time, he was elected bishop of Milan by popular acclaim in A.D. 373. He was one of the most influential bishops of his time, a famous preacher, and a champion of orthodox faith. It was he who baptized Saint Augustine in 387.

Aphrahat, or Aphraates, the first of the Syriac Church Fathers. He was an ascetic, living in the early fourth century, and is sometimes called the Persian Sage. He wrote a series of Demonstrations on the Christian Faith.

Saint Augustine: born at Tagaste in North Africa in 354, but not baptized until he was 33 years old, after one of the most famous conversions in the history of the Church. Became bishop of Hippo in North Africa in 396, and engaged in many doctrinal controversies. His influence on Western theology is immense.

Saint Chromatius, bishop of Aquileia in North Italy from 388 to 407. Friend and contemporary of Saint Ambrose and Saint John Chrysostom.

Saint John Chrysostom, c. 347 to 407. Served as deacon and priest at Antioch, where his preaching gained him the name Chrysostom, "golden-mouthed." Made bishop of Constantinople in 398, where he worked hard to reform the court, clergy, and people; but his enemies secured his banishment in 404, and he died from ill treatment on the journey.

Saint Cyprian, a pagan rhetorician converted to Christianity about the year 246. Two years later elected bishop of Carthage in North Africa, just before the outbreak of persecution under Decius. He had to deal with the problem of the reconciliation of the many Christians who had lapsed under the persecution, as well as the question of rebaptism of heretics. He died a martyr's death in the persecution of Valerian in 258.

Saint Cyril, bishop of Jerusalem from about 349 to 386. He was several times banished for his opposition to Arianism. His Catechetical Lectures have the special interest of having been delivered at the very site of our Lord's Passion and Resurrection, and they throw light on the Palestinian liturgy of the fourth century.

Didymus the Blind, an Alexandrian theologian born about 313. He directed the Catechetical School at Alexandria.

Quodvultdeus, bishop of Carthage in the fifth century. For a long time the sermons now attributed to him were ascribed to Saint Prosper or Saint Augustine; they are included among Saint Augustine's sermons in Migne.

Theodore of Mopsuestia, born at Antioch about 350, where he studied with his friend Saint John Chrysostom. In 392 he was made bishop of Mopsuestia, and gained a reputation for theological learning. He has been harshly judged and some of his writings condemned, but the recovery of some of his works in modern times has shown that such condemnation was unmerited.

Tertullian, one of the earliest of the Latin Fathers. He was born about 160 in Carthage, and was converted to Christianity before 197. His writings were brilliant but very polemical. His language and thought had a great influence on Western theology; but his rigorist inclinations eventually caused him to join the Montanist sect.

Sarapion, bishop of Thmuis in Egypt from about 339, the friend and contemporary of Saint Athanasius and Saint Antony.

Saint Zeno, bishop of Verona from A.D. 362. We owe to him a series of short sermons on the symbolism of the baptismal rites.

Glossary

Apostles' Creed: This is the earliest creed used by the Church. It was in common use in baptismal teaching in the Western Church, to which Augustine (from whose writings most of the section on the Creed is taken) belonged. While less complete than the Nicene Creed (the accepted creed of the Eastern Church), the Apostles' Creed is acknowledged as valid throughout Christendom.

baptism: The early Church regarded baptism as the act in which one became a Christian. It was mandatory for anyone who wished to participate fully in the life of the Church.

Bright Week: The week after Easter (here called Easter week) is referred to in the Orthodox Church as Bright Week, and in Western liturgical churches as the Easter octave.

catechetical instruction: Instruction in the essential doctrines and practices of the Christian Faith, given to prepare converts for baptism.

catechetics: The science of catechetical instruction.

catechist: A teacher responsible for delivering catechetical instruction.

catechumen: A convert who has not yet been baptized. In this text the term may refer either to one who has enrolled for baptism, or to one who has not yet done so.

catechumenate: A group of catechumens; also, the process of undergoing catechetical instruction.

charisms: Spiritual gifts.

chrismation: The sacrament of anointing with oil to seal one's baptism. In the Western Church this is referred to as confirmation.

Eucharist: The sacrament of the Lord's Supper or Holy Communion.

eucharistic liturgy: The primary liturgical service of the Church, including the sacrament of the Eucharist. In the Western Church this is referred to as the Mass; in the Orthodox Church it is called the Divine Liturgy.

exorcisms: The practice of performing exorcisms on all baptismal candidates does not imply that the Church believed they were all actually demon-possessed. However, all humans who have not been baptized are under the devil's power, as will be explained later on.

fasting: In the early Church (and in the Orthodox Church today), various forms of fasting were practiced. During all of Lent and at certain other times, the faithful abstained from certain categories of foods, including meat, dairy products, fish, wine, and oil. Certain days, such as the Friday and Saturday before Easter, were designated as days of *strict* fasting; on these days the faithful did not eat or drink anything at all.

footwashing: Footwashing was sometimes practiced on Holy Thursday as well as during the baptismal rites, in imitation of the Lord washing the disciples' feet at the Last Supper.

Lent: A forty-day period of fasting, intensified prayer, almsgiving, and repentance preceding Easter (Pascha).

liturgy: Either (a) a general term for any of the prescribed services of the Church; or (b) a term referring specifically to the eucharistic liturgy.

Liturgy of the Word: The first part of the eucharistic liturgy, including intercessory prayers, hymns, and scripture readings; called the Synaxis in the Orthodox Church.

mysteries: Another term for sacraments, reflecting the fact that the action of the grace of God in the sacraments cannot be fully apprehended by the human mind.

novitiate: A period of preparation for being admitted as a full member of a monastic community.

Pascha: In the Orthodox Church, Easter is referred to as Pascha, a word which derives from the Greek word for Passover.

sacraments: The seven formal rites of the Church in which grace is conveyed to the participants. In the early Church these included baptism, chrismation, the Eucharist, confession, marriage, ordination, and holy unction (anointing for healing).

sponsors: A sponsor for an adult catechumen is equivalent to a godparent for a child. The sponsor undertakes to guide and encourage the new Christian in his or her faith.

vigils: A vigil consists of a night spent in prayer, usually in a church. On certain holy days a special vigil service takes place, but vigils may also be kept individually. Often those keeping vigil will chant or read through the Psalter.

About the Author

Sister Anne Field O.S.B. is a Roman Catholic, a native of the English Midlands, and has been a member of the Benedictine community at Stanbrook Abbey, Worcester, for the past forty-eight years. Among other assignments in the monastery she worked for a number of years on translating patristic texts for the Monastic Lectionary, and is at present engaged in the production of revised books for the choral Offices in the abbey church.